Literature and the Science of the Unknowable

Gina Crocenzi

Literature and the Science of the Unknowable

Julia Kristeva and Gaston Bachelard

Lambert Academic Publishing

Impressum/Imprint (nur für Deutschland/ only for Germany)
Bibliografische Information der Deutschen Nationalbibliothek: Die Deutsche Nationalbibliothek verzeichnet diese Publikation in der Deutschen Nationalbibliografie; detaillierte bibliografische Daten sind im Internet über http://dnb.d-nb.de abrufbar.
Alle in diesem Buch genannten Marken und Produktnamen unterliegen warenzeichen-, marken- oder patentrechtlichem Schutz bzw. sind Warenzeichen oder eingetragene Warenzeichen der jeweiligen Inhaber. Die Wiedergabe von Marken, Produktnamen, Gebrauchsnamen, Handelsnamen, Warenbezeichnungen u.s.w. in diesem Werk berechtigt auch ohne besondere Kennzeichnung nicht zu der Annahme, dass solche Namen im Sinne der Warenzeichen- und Markenschutzgesetzgebung als frei zu betrachten wären und daher von jedermann benutzt werden dürften.

Verlag: Lambert Academic Publishing AG & Co. KG
Dudweiler Landstr. 99, 66123 Saarbrücken, Deutschland
Telefon +49 681 3720-310, Telefax +49 681 3720-3109, Email: info@lap-publishing.com

Herstellung in Deutschland:
Schaltungsdienst Lange o.H.G., Berlin
Books on Demand GmbH, Norderstedt
Reha GmbH, Saarbrücken
Amazon Distribution GmbH, Leipzig
ISBN: 978-3-8383-0757-2

Imprint (only for USA, GB)
Bibliographic information published by the Deutsche Nationalbibliothek: The Deutsche Nationalbibliothek lists this publication in the Deutsche Nationalbibliografie; detailed bibliographic data are available in the Internet at http://dnb.d-nb.de.
Any brand names and product names mentioned in this book are subject to trademark, brand or patent protection and are trademarks or registered trademarks of their respective holders. The use of brand names, product names, common names, trade names, product descriptions etc. even without a particular marking in this works is in no way to be construed to mean that such names may be regarded as unrestricted in respect of trademark and brand protection legislation and could thus be used by anyone.

Publisher:
Lambert Academic Publishing AG & Co. KG
Dudweiler Landstr. 99, 66123 Saarbrücken, Germany
Phone +49 681 3720-310, Fax +49 681 3720-3109, Email: info@lap-publishing.com

Copyright © 2009 Lambert Academic Publishing AG & Co. KG and licensors
All rights reserved. Saarbrücken 2009

Printed in the U.S.A.
Printed in the U.K. by (see last page)
ISBN: 978-3-8383-0757-2

TABLE OF CONTENTS

Introduction..4

PART I

JULIA KRISTEVA

Chapter

    1. THE "PROCESS" OF TRUTH …..9

    2. THE FRENCH CONNECTION: MICHEL SERRES, ILYA PRIGOGINE, ET AL …..15

    3. THE KRISTEVAN ABSOLUTE: IMMANENT TRANSCENDENCE …..30

    4. ART OR SCIENCE? …...44

    5. GOD AND THE ABSOLUTE...58

    6. POLITICS AND TRANSCENDENCE 62

    7. LANGUAGE AND THE ABSOLUTE 66

    8. THE ABSOLUTE AS SUBLIME …..80

PART II
GASTON BACHELARD

Chapter

9. SCIENCE AND LITERATURE - *ANIMUS* AND *ANIMA* 90

10. THE EPISTEMOLOGY OF THE ABSOLUTE...................94

11. ABSOLUTE OF APPROXIMATION............................101

12. ABSOLUTE AS DYNAMIC PROCESS......................105

13. EPISTEMOLOGICAL REVOLUTION 111

14. DIALECTICAL ABSOLUTE 119

15. REASON AND REVERIE 127

16. FROM SCIENCE TO POETRY 128

17. INTERTEXTUALITY: RETURN TO RATIONALISM............134

18. TEMPERED RATIONALISM 147

19. SCIENCE AND POETRY 154

PART III
SEARCH FOR A FINAL THEORY

Chapter

20. ORDER OUT OF CHAOS...............................160

21 SACRED SCIENCE 177

22 BEAUTIFUL DREAMER.......................................185

CONCLUSION..190
BIBLIOGRAPHY 198

INTRODUCTION

Much of post-modern philosophy and literary theory has dismissed the metaphysical category of the Absolute as "[Being] in the sense of the true."[1] Where metaphysics saw truth as absolute "disclosure" or "unconcealment"[2] of the fullness of being, Nietzsche's jubilant obituary ("God is dead") made way for the dark side of the Absolute: restless, unstructured negativity and the eclipse of reason. And in philosophy's wake followed a redefining of the concept of truth by literature, science, theology and the arts, no longer a mimesis of what has already been 'presented,'[3] no longer a recollection of the revealed Word, but rather an auto-genetic play of dichotomous impulses: reason and being, essence and existence, object and subject, transcendence and immanence. The literature of the avant-garde is an unleashing of what Western metaphysical categories had kept at bay - a revolt against the reductive, 'either-or' dualities of rationalism and an assertion of the rightful stature of difference and alterity within the very rubric of truth.

---

1 Heidegger, "The Question of Being," <u>Basic Writings</u> (New York: Harper & Row, 1975), p. 13.
2 Heidegger. "the End of Philosophy and the Task of Thinking. <u>Basic Writings</u> (New York: Harper & Row, 1975). p. 388.

3 Cf. Derrida's qualification of the "metaphysics of presence".....

Both Bachelard and Kristeva embrace such "negativity" in all of its capacity to found new possibilities of intellect and spirit. Kristeva celebrates the revalorization of the drives and their hypothetical construct, the "semiotic," celebrating it for its creativity in the process of the subject's development as well as its proclivity to destabilize, even aggravate the status quo. The primacy she assigns to negativity and the body in signification (i.e., constructing meaning) run counter to the metaphysical presuppositions of the Enlightenment tradition, whereby the thinking subject channels bodily instinct in deference to a rational Absolute. Yet Kristeva's eclipsing of the Hegelian Absolute is less a categorical denial of the quiddity of absolute transcendence than a commitment to rethink the notion of truth in light of post-modern developments. While her position on the status of the Absolute vacillates throughout her writings, ultimately she maintains a firm conviction that there is still an indispensable role for a revamped metaphysics in the modern era.

In a similar vein, Bachelard's call for an "applied rationalism"--a philosophy of science that is more faithful to the findings of modern physics--is a re-appraisal of the reigning epistemologies (Newtonian physics, empiricism, positivism) in light of relativity and the disturbing role of uncertainty in modern science. Yet Bachelard's work as well is far from a lapse into solipsism and radical relativity. His psycho-literary theory of the "oneiric" and of archetypal, poetic truth are not only a ratification of the Absolute but an avowal that human existence cannot achieve full integrity unless the rational *(animus)* and the intuitive *(anima)* are upheld in a mutually compatible yet dialectical interplay.

The revolt of modern literature and philosophy against the notion of an absolute principle that determines human identity and its modes of knowing is recapitulated in post-Einsteinian physics. Whereas classical physics acknowledged the universe as a structure whose rational workings science could decode and whose harmony was grounded in an omniscient Final Cause, modern cosmology introduced such self-effacing concepts as "error", "uncertainty", "relativity", and "chaos". Scientific truth, it was declared, no less than metaphysical and literary truth, is not absolute. Physics does not enact a mimetic reproduction of the flawless rationality of Nature, in anticipation of an ultimate "end of science." Rather, it is the state of the "intertextuality" of a questioning subject oriented toward an inexhaustible reality that 'produces' him inasmuch as he comes to know it. Subject and object of modern science are no longer bound by the epistemological fields of empiricism. Truth is not revealed by a divine transcendence, nor is it the by-product of immutable principles issued by a supreme Absolute. Scientific theories do not disclose the a priori truths of Reason; rather, they propose hypothetical models that appear truthful to the observer in a particular arrangement of phenomena largely, if not solely, as a result of the instruments and methodology of the reigning paradigm. Whether or not modern physics suspends the question of metaphysics, thereby bracketing the idea of the Absolute, or offers an alternative transcendence compatible with post-modern literature and critical theory is the subject of this dissertation.

PART I

JULIA KRISTEVA

CHAPTER ONE: THE "PROCESS" OF TRUTH

Literature and science have emerged out of the Western episteme as two distinct "cultures"[4], each diametrically opposed to the other with respect to what constitutes truth, knowledge and language. The discipline of science has come to represent a bastion of rational truth, guaranteed by propositions that conform to reality. Scientific discourse is strictly mimetic; the couplet of theory and method corresponds to increasingly accurate depictions of experience. The literary text, as it has been conceived since the romantic movement, presumes to be but one of several elements that problematize meaning – a complex dynamic of author, audience, process. Modern literature does not add to a canon of "eternal truth,[5] but takes part in the spontaneous play of the written word by enriching the diachronic pattern of meaning that is the emergent text.

The division of "literature" and "science" into distinct disciplines reflects a more fundamental difference which becomes unmistakably apparent in the Romantic era. Yet in antiquity and in the Middle Ages, literature and science were categorized as different curricula both guaranteed by the timeless authority of the text:

---

[4] C.P. Snow, The Two Cultures and the Scientific Revolution (Cambridge,1959), p. 16.
[5] W.R. Paulson, The Noise of Culture (Ithaca: Cornell University Press, 1988), p. 4.

> The respect inspired by the text sets the text in the place of the object....it is not the book of nature that is read, but the book instead of nature; not the human body, but the Canon of Avicenna; no longer human language, but Priscian; not the universe, but Aristotle is read; not the sky, but Ptolemy.[6]

Literature, no less than science, was ratified by its ability to enlighten the reader to the basic tenets of immutable, logocentric truth.

The advent of observational and experimental science challenged the dogmatic acceptance of received truths and resulted in such infamous controversies as Galileo's condemnation by the Catholic Church. If intellect questioned the "institutional habits" (Paulson, 9) of the status quo, it was to be highly suspect at best. Not until the Romantic era does the modern notion of expansive, self-generative writing come into being. Here, most explicitly, does the poet object to the "water-wheels of Newton...with cogs tyrannic moving by compulsion each other."[7] Shelley, in his "Defense of Poetry", mourns the degradation of man who, "...having enslaved the elements, remains himself a

---

[6] Eugenio Garin. L'Education de l'homme moderne. Paris, 1968, p. 67. Garin refers here to medieval education.
[7] William Blake, "Jerusalem," The Portable Blake. Ed. Alfred Kazin. New York, 1976, p. 463.

slave. "[8] The romantics upset the Kantian order of noumena-phenomena and declared that which is unobservable, imperceptible, to be of ultimate truth.

The Jena group, advocates of the romantic conception of literature who established the short-lived literary review "Athenaeum", called for an ecumenical reconciliation of art and science. Their mantra became an ode to unity: "...all art should become science and all science art; poetry and philosophy should be made one."[9] Writing becomes philosophy, or science, *par excellence*, for it is acutely conscious of the new knowledge it produces, all the while reveling in its own wit and "organic spirit."[10] No longer seen as rivals in the quest for truth, science and literature are mutually devoted to the enrichment of the spirit.

In 1926, English literary critic I. A. Richards suggested in his Science and Poetry that poetry has an ontological status that sets it apart from science. Rather than producing statements that are true "by force of logic" and denotation, poetry simply "is."[11] Furthermore, where science has eradicated many of the ghosts of superstition that stemmed from ignorance of the natural

---
8 Percy B. Shelley, Shelley's Prose, ed. D. L. Clark, Albuquerque, 1954, p. 293.
9 Friedrich Schlegel, "Critical Fragment 115," "Lucinde" and the Fragments. Trans. P. Firchow, Minneapolis, 1971, p. 157.
10 Ibid, p. 221.
11 I.A. Richards, Science and Poetry, New York: Norton, 1926, pp. 34-35.

world, poetry reserves a space for validating what science has discredited. It responds to a need to imagine, to hope, to believe in what cannot be directly observed:

> The remedy... is to cut our pseudo-statements free from belief and yet retain them, in this released (poetic) state, as the main instruments by which we order our attitudes to one another and to the world.[12]

Poetry is the cathartic medium for an unleashing of the "play of interests" (Paulson, 18), which the mind seeks to bring into balance with knowledge and understanding.

Structuralism offers instead a model of the literary text that insists on the autonomy of textual meaning. Roland Barthes and his fellow semiologists refused to acknowledge that literature communicates a "truth about something other than itself" (Paulson, 19), seeing it rather as a producer of newly self-created truth. It is in the status they grant to logos, Barthes argues, that science and literature differ. Science, he claims, is didactic; the language of science is a vehicle for encoding a pre-established message. Modern technocratic society accepts these truths
without question, and becomes indifferent to the inherently problematic

---
[12] Richards, p. 72.

nature of language:

> Science hides what for Barthes is a fundamental truth of
> language, one that literature assumes: there is
> no meaning completely outside of language, no
> signified that transcends the realm of signs.[13]

Barthes takes up the torch of Jena: science must become more literary in its use of language, this time in order to dismantle the "hierarchical and totalitarian"(19) presumptions of its own discourse.

Yet semiology has opened Pandora's box: if the text is no longer to submit itself to a priori truths: if, as deconstruction would have it, the truth of language is "to deny the existence of truths preceding or external to language" (25): if literature is nothing but a statement on language's own futility and impotence, then is not the literary word reduced to a nihilistic wasteland – a proliferation of signs signifying nothing?

Derrida would beg to differ. In the wake of Nietzsche's pronouncement of the death of God, he announces the closure of Western metaphysics. He grants that certain types of discourse are indeed grounded on metaphysical

---
13 Paulson, p. 20.

presuppositions and that their meaning can be deduced from those premises. But aside from that metaphysical paradigm, there exist other conceptions of meaning. Derrida is in effect

> ...calling into question a particular representation of what it is to mean: the notion of a sense completely separable from language and signs, existing in the consciousness or imagination of the author before being "put into" words.[14]

Post-structuralist literary theory rejects the metaphysics of presence as sole purveyor of truth, discrediting the viability of an absolute correspondence between word and reality, logos and being.

---

14 Paulson, p. 27.

CHAPTER TWO: THE FRENCH CONNECTION: MICHEL SERRES, ILYA PRIGOGINE, et al.

Medieval science and literature were separated only by curricular classification. By the time of the scientific era they had been polarized by conflicting claims to objective truth. Romanticism took exception to the primacy of reason, declaring literature to be the revelation of the Absolute and science to be the ultimate non-truth of a mechanized, utilitarian society. The modern age, on the other hand, has witnessed an emerging mutuality and interdependence between the epistemological models of both literature and science. Echoing both the creed of the Jena group and the literary metaphysics of Bachelard, scientific knowledge, "awakened from the dreams of an inspired revelation, can now discover itself to be both a 'poetic listening' to nature and a natural process within nature...."[15] Theoretical biologist Francisco Varela remarks that "our knowledge, including science, can be accurately empirical and experimental, without requiring for it the claim of solidity or fixed reference." [16]There can be meaning, as Derrida proffered, without an unquestioning acceptance of pre-established, external truths.

---

15 IlyaPrigogine and Isabelle Stengers, La Nouvelle Alliance: Metamorphose de la science (Paris: Gallimard, 1979, p. 296.
16 Francisco Varela, Principles of Biological Autonomy. (New York: Elsevier North-Holland, 1979), p. 277.

As we shall see, the truth of the Kristevan "symbolic" (language, reason) comes into being only within the context of the dialectical relationship to its artful, (corporeal) alter ego: the "semiotic." For Kristeva, neither the language of reason--the denotative transcript of consciousness -- nor the language of the drives --the sensual traces of our material being — has ontological priority. Michel Serres, philosopher and historian of sciences, develops the self-same assertion that the faculty of the imagination and its literary counterpart are as truthful as the "supposedly rigorous discourses of the sciences" (Paulson, 31). The "figural" (Paulson, 31) knowledge that the imaginary word communicates in literature is both "accessible and profound,...without theory, without awkward weight, not boring but intelligent...." [17] The 'clarity and distinctness' of science generate a form of truth that is predisposed to seek "the extrema of order and universal method" (Paulson, 36). Yet its claims to ultimate truth (e.g., empiricism, positivism, etc.) eclipse those paradigms of knowing that incorporate complexity, chaos, and uncertainty. This bifurcation of reason and imagination is a contrived separation; for science, he claims, is "not necessarily a matter of unity or of order: multiplicity and noise are not necessarily on the irrational side."[18]

---

17 Michel Serres, The Parasite, trans. L.R. Schehr, Baltimore, 1982, p. 6.

18 Serres, Genese, Paris, 1982, p. 241.

Serres envisages a literary culture that is truth-seeking and a scientific culture that is less driven by totalitarian, "ahistorical laws" (Paulson, 36). Yet his holistic approach to science and literature is far from a synthetic leveling of differences between the two. As Paulson explains, what Serres is calling for is neither radical disciplinary autonomy nor "...abstracting schemas for integrating different fields of inquiry, but passages from one domain to the other..."(36-37). Serres' call for a nonlinear reciprocity between literature and science is reminiscent of Bachelard's eclectic blending of philosophy of science, literary theory, Jungian psychology, and poetry. It is likewise evocative of Kristeva's psychology of the emergent self as dialectically processed by both body and mind, art and science.

For both modern science and literary theory, truth is a process brought into being by heterogeneous elements that are authenticated at every level, not only at the conscious stage. Observer and observed, subject and object, are "wrought by a shared division more stable and potent than their antique separation: they are, together, order and disorder...."[19] Knowledge is wrought in the interstices of body, mind, and culture; there is a cognitive role not just for language and social structures, but for "biological and physical structures as well." [20] Serres' consideration of new paradigms of meaning or order in both literature and science

---

19 Serres, Hermes: Literature, Science, Philosophy, eds. D. F. Bell and J. V. Harari, Baltimore, Johns Hopkins, 1982.

20 Serres suggests that we already have a theory about what happens in the exchange between the two levels: psychoanalysis. What we call the unconscious - slips, dreams, neurotic symptoms - is a "source of potentially information producing noise....for our consciousness." Paulson, 49.

radically alters the orthodox distinctions between them. He proposes an analogy between the "noise" of information in complex, nonlinear systems and the residue of the literary text which resists reduction to rational terms. Just as the classical notion of "mimesis"—truth as reflection of an external, universal order-has been replaced by the post-modern theory of truth as polysemic, so information science introduces the notion that "randomness is a kind of order, if it can be made meaningful...."[21] With Serres, the French communications specialist Abraham Moles distinguishes between the crisp, noise-free communication of utilitarian language, and literary communication which "assumes its noise as a constitutive factor of itself" (Paulson, 83). In poetry, for example, what is expressed is not reducible to the denotative word; "...what is received is not exactly what was sent" (83), to put it in the jargon of information science. If one understands and accepts that chaos for modern science does not detract from truth, but in fact contributes to a truth of a different kind—"self-organization from noise" (Paulson, 85)—then one can welcome a complementary theory of the literary text as signifying truth in a non-representational discourse:

> The poetic text begins as an attempt to go beyond the usual system of a language – in which the word is a conventional sign – to a specifically artistic system, in which sounds, rhythms, and positional relations between elements will signify in new ways. [22]

The "noise" of the literary text is precisely that indeterminate meaning, an

---

21 Henri Atlan, "Disorder, Complexity, and Meaning," Disorder and Order. Ed P. Livingston, Stanford, 1984, p. 110. Atlan defines meaning as "the effect of some information transmitted any channel of communication."
22 Junj Lotman, "The Structure of the Artistic Text," Trans. G. Lenhoff and R. Vroon. Michigan Slavic Contributions 7, 1977, p. 75.

irrecoverable "residue...that cannot be resolved by grammatical means," and which reconstitutes literary truth as "aleatory" (Paulson, 88).[23] Insofar as the reader of modern literature must reconfigure his traditional posture of receiver of a transmitted message, he must accommodate and interpret noise, ambiguity, and interference. The truth of a text is derivative organization "out of chaos" (Paulson, 91), and the ambiguity and non-sense of the text is not to be dismissed as "muddled prose" (Paulson, 90) but, as de Man puts it, "aporias (that) become the very meaning of literary texts" (Paulson, 92).

---

[23] "aleatory" - other.

The challenge of modern literature and critical theory is to demythologize literary studies as they have been traditionally conceived. Humanism, in keeping with the hard sciences, must reject the conception of meaning or truth as "a message...sent by the author...or by the text itself considered as object of observation" (Paulson, 94). The irreducible "residue" of meaning that resists monolithic, authorial interpretation revalorizes ambiguity as...

> ...a positive factor in an unforeseen organizational complexity, rather than simply a negative factor inhibiting the transmission of pre-established information.[24]

Just as noise, chaos and unpredictability act as newfound indicators of unknown probable truth, so ambiguity and noise, in the language of the text, become the harbingers of an a posteriori literary truth. In the same way that unstable, noisy transmission is now known to be "rarely altogether lost" (96), but rather accessible to the receiver by other communicative means, so the disorder of the text divulges a rich panoply of unexplored possible meanings.

The modern text, for Serres, is neither a purveyor of transmitted truths nor an object for formal analysis. It is rather a discourse that solicits our

---

[24] Paulson, p. 95.

"attunement"[25] to a process of questioning that, far from uncovering a message, suggests limitless methods of interpretation:

> ...it brings us some specific verbal material unlike anything we know, which is thus incapable of being completely integrated into the schemas we already had for knowing; the text leads us to modify ourselves, to shift position, to change and adapt our ways of mind a little so that it can become a part of them.[26]

The alterity - the non-sense—of literary language can become meaningful for us precisely because we are fascinated by and receptive to the unknown. The element of the text that is "radically different" (99) presents itself as no less a "dilemma" (103) than the mystifying noise of non-linear systems.

Literature is neither a radical counterculture whose only function is to console a society overrun by "cold and calculating scientists" (102), nor a relic to be admired for its didactic and aesthetic properties. It is the literary gadfly, stimulating the mind to consider new perspectives, new possibilities, new "dilemmas" (103) that classical literary theory discounted as subversive or senseless.

---

[25] The Heideggerian term "Stimmung" is translated as "attunement" or a "bringing into accord". We are "attuned" to being as a whole, according to Heidegger, when we are in a comportment of "letting beings be", at the same time recognizing that the "whole of being" – the Absolute – always remains concealed. Heidegger, Basic Writings, New York, Harper & Row, 1977, p. 134.
[26] Paulson, p. 99.

In 1977 Belgian scientist Ilya Prigogine received the Nobel Prize in chemistry for study of "dissipative structures."[27] His analysis of self-organizing systems, which by definition do not conform to the laws of equilibrium thermodynamics, concludes that the fluctuations of open systems render them ripe for "spontaneous self-organization, ruptures of symmetry, (and) evolutions towards growing complexity and diversity."[28] Prigogine makes an unusual comparison between the scientist's authentication of noise and randomness to:

> ...the poetic listening to nature - in the etymological sense in which the poet is a maker - an active, manipulating and calculating exploration, but henceforth capable of respecting the nature whose voice it brings forth.[29]

Science's 'listening' to the noise of dissipative structures requires both an active vigilance and a willing acquiescence to the opacity of ultimate truth.

The experimental barriers that dissipative structures entail do not, however, pose limits for predictability. On the contrary, claims Prigogine, the un-observability of such systems forces the scientist to confront the inexplicable and confess a new "appreciation of the random and the unpredictable" (Paulson, 107). The inclusion of unpredictability in theories of self-organization

---

[27] Paulson defines these structures as those whose "existence depends on the continueal expenditure or dissipation of energy that keeps it away from thermodynamic equilibrium." p. 105
[28] Prigogine and Stengers, p. 271.
[29] Prigogine and Stengers, p. 281.

invites controversy from mathematicians such as Rene Thom, who label Prigogine and his colleagues as "betrayers of the scientific ideal of deterministic, reproducible, and...universally consensual knowledge" (106). Thom warns that any ratification of chance in the scientific enterprise is likewise an affirmation that "there are natural phenomena which we shall never be able to describe, therefore never understand."[30] Science, he counsels, must reject the "aleatory"[31] and persist in the zealous "conquest"[32] of empirical verification. Thom is guilty, Prigogine responds, of his own metaphysical presupposition—that the laws of determinism are the only objective, discoverable laws. On the contrary, the object of science is not only that which can be observed and predicted, but that which is revealed partially, through statistical operations. Cognition is not only a linear process of induction culminating in total knowledge, but may also incorporate "ignorance" and "a discontinuity...between the parts and the whole" (Paulson, 108).[33]

In self-organizing systems, the one-to-one correspondence between subject (observer) and object (observed) is entirely reconfigured. What is noisy confusion at one level of observation may appear as information when it is "reconstituted as input to the observer's construction of a global

---

[30] Rene Thom, "Stop Chance! Silence Noise!," trans F. Chumbles, SubStance. no. 40, 1983, p. 11.
[31] Precisely what Bachelard and Kristeva seek to reintroduce within the category of meaning.
[32] Thom, p. 20.
[33] On the implications of complexity, see Isabelle Stengers, "Decouvrir la Complexite," pp. 223-254, in Ordres et Desordres: Enquete sur un Nouveau Paradigme. Paris, 1982.

explanation of how (one level) fits into the larger system" (Paulson, 110). The very act of knowing is elevated to a multi-level process of synthetic interpretation; it is not simply a matter of the subject unraveling the observed level at hand, but of proposing a creative hypothesis explaining how this immediate level can be "integrated into the overall system" (110). This comprehensive operation of cognition suggests a far more intuitive heuristic approach than the classical boundaries of empirical science would have allowed. Just as the interpreter of literary complexity can no longer impose a grid of conceptual tools that unlocks textual meaning, so the scientist must suspend absolute mastery of a dissipative structure until what is initial noise can become "an ingredient of a new level of explanation" (Paulson, 111).

Multi-level systems are not to be confused with hierarchical or pyramid structures, which integrate lower levels of understanding into progressively higher organizing principles. The relations among different levels of a system are not evaluated in all their complexity until the knower has "(assimilated) ... the radically new, the exceptional" (112). No juxtaposition of cognitive levels can produce a completely new coherence which is more than just the sum of its parts. And no singular theoretical construct in a text can account for the polysystemic coherence of the text:

>   The intersection of different levels, different
>   features of language, or different mimetic projections

> within a text is not fully disciplined by pre-established rules; it must be found out and ultimately constructed by the reader, who possesses considerable knowledge of linguistic and cultural codes ...but who must literally discover *the autonomous codes by which a given text is itself organized.*[34] (italics mine)

Information science, in its study of open systems, is increasingly receptive to "interdisciplinarity from within" (Paulson, 114). What was once the static, experimentally verifiable 'object' of empirical science is now a product of multiple encounters with different levels of reality, shifting parts of a speculated totality that is unknowable in and of itself. Just as the modern text is but prologue to an emergent yet receding truth,[35] belonging to "no totality that we can conceive" (115), so the object of science conceals itself as a "strange object" (115). Romanticism's manifesto, Fragment 116 of the <u>Athenaeum,</u> proclaims for poetry the same status of perpetual becoming and inexhaustibility that complexity and self-organizing systems profess for modern science: "***poiesis*** itself" (Paulson, 118).[36]

---

34 Paulson, p. 114.
35 The prototypical modern text, according to Schlegel, is "...forever becoming and never...perfected. It can be exhausted by no theory." "Lucinde and the Fragments", pp. 175-176.
36 The comparison between Romantic poetry and self-organizing systems is not a flawless one. As Paulson puts it, "There is an undeniable relation between the literary interpretation of ...organization from noise and the romantic postulate of the organicity of a work of art, although this relation cannot be reduced to an identity.", p. 119.

Modern biology resembles information science in its depiction of living organization as "autopoiesis (-)...self- production or self-creation" (Paulson, 121). The Santiago school of theoretical biology, led by Humberto Maturana and Francisco Varela, presents an interdisciplinary critique of the classical realist paradigm. The traditional approach to epistemology in the social and life sciences, they claim, has been "representationist" (123). Knowledge, or information, is defined as a "correspondence between symbolic units in one structure and symbolic units in another structure."[37] While this model may work for lower-level systems, the "inputs and outputs" (Paulson, 122) of the representationist perspective, they find, proves inadequate when applied to higher-level biological systems, such as the immune and nervous systems. Such complex systems are better understood as autonomous structures that maintain their own organizational identity in the face of fluctuations from the environment:

> In the (representationist model) ...interactions from the environment are instructive, constitute part of the definition of the system's organization...in the autonomy interpretation, the environment is seen as a source of perturbations independent of the definition of the system's organization, and hence intrinsically noninstructive *(sic):* they can trigger, but not determine, the course of transformation...in
>
> (the former case)...an input...specifies the system's organization and structure: in (the latter case) a perturbation participates

---

37 Varela, p xiv.

in the transformation of an independently specified system.[38]

For the autonomous structures of the life sciences, no less than for the *poiesis* of the literary text, truth is an emergent unfolding of indiscriminate levels of being. The determination of meaning is never the function of an over-arching, absolute structure.[39]

As we shall see in the Kristevan model of the psyche, the indeterminacy of autopoietic systems in a dynamic state of self-production vis-a-vis outside structures and processes results in a more authentic, albeit problematic theory of the truth of human subjectivity. And, in keeping with Bachelard's notion of an archetypal meta-language, we shall see how literary language derives its own a priori "internal, self-referential laws....which are not those of the message one seeks to send through it" (Paulson, 130). Our conventional manipulation of language as a "communicative instrument" (130) remains questionable at best. The opacity of the literary word continues to tease,

---

38 Varela, pp. 261-262.

39 It is vital to note that the critical model of Varela and Maturana is at home in neither the representational approach – the text as a "vehicle of transmission....of a reality external to it." (Paulson, 124) -- nor the autonomy perspective, which interprets the text as self-referentially structured. The Santiago school distinguishes "autopoietic systems" from autonomous systems in the way the processes determine their components and in the way those same components in turn constitute the system's structural identity. (Varela, p. 13.)

baffle, bemuse and frustrate, as a result of "the ambiguities, overlappings, and uncertainties" (130) that are the inherent properties of language.

Just as Bachelard enlightens the reader of poetry to the archetypal images that give the text its composite meaning, and just as Kristeva re-evaluates psychoanalysis and literary criticism as open-ended exchanges between process and product, subject and object, so science's autonomous systems profess no "unchanging truth" toward which knowledge converges, but an "active, independent, autonomous construction of meaning" (Paulson, 139). The incorporation of risk, disorder, and noise in the production of scientific knowledge is a necessary evil both at the microscopic level and at complex levels of biological organization:

> ...this kind of negotiation with disorder...is the only kind of knowledge accessible to us, because we are not the disincarnated observers postulated by early modern science but beings belonging to the world that we try to understand. And this world, unlike the...predictable universe postulated by scientific determinism, is an open world, one in which the unpredictable appearance of the new is not irrational. Knowledge, in this context, entails risk and dialogue, not mechanisms for ensuring maximal certainty.... [40]

There is an element of the unknown, the transcendent, which develops out of

---
40 Paulson, p. 143.

reason's encounter with disorder. It is this very obstruction of meaning, this unpredictability, that compels the knower to consider new meanings "beyond whatever could be said to have been communicated" (145). Science's recognition of noncontinuous, nonpredictable, self-organizing systems is an implicit endorsement of the increasingly seminal role of literature in the information age. The inherent value of literary discourse to an informational society lies not in its communicability or in what philosopher Jean-Francois Lyotard calls "performativity", but in its "paralogical innovation:" the production of novel concepts that generate intellectual invention and innovation.[41] In my analysis of the literary and psychological criticism of Kristeva, and of the philosophy of science and poetics of Bachelard, I will examine how each one theorizes the quintessentially modern dilemma of absolute truth in an era of rational and artistic uncertainty. I will attempt to show how each presents a novel perspective on the complicity of reason and imagination in light of recently redefined notions of truth in scientific and literary discourse.

---

[41] Jean Francois Lyotard. The Postmodern Condition, trans. G. Bennington and B. Massumi. University of Minnesota Press, 1984, p. 41.

CHAPTER THREE

THE KRISTEVAN ABSOLUTE: IMMANENT TRANSCENDENCE

In 1966, at the age of 25, Julia Kristeva arrived in Paris for a doctoral research fellowship. By Spring of 1967 her articles were already appearing in the most celebrated intellectual journals: *Critique, Langages,* and Tel Quel. The publication of her dissertation on semiotics, "La Revolution du langage poetique," in 1974 catapulted her to success in the literary circles of the Left Bank and enabled her to earn a chair in linguistics at the University of Paris VII.

After working with fellow Bulgarian Tzvetan Todorov and structuralist Lucien Goldmann, Kristeva studied under Roland Barthes. Barthes, who has remained the most influential of her teachers, reviews Kristeva's first publication, Semeiotike:

> .....Kristeva changes the order of things: she always destroys the latest preconception, the one we thought we could be comforted by....what she displaces is the already-said [sic], that is to say, the insistence of the signified; what she subverts is *the authority of* monologic science... [italics mine] [42]

---

[42] Roland Barthes, "L'Etrangere," La Quinzaine Litteraire, 94, 1-15, May (1970), p. 19.

Kristeva's iconoclastic *tour-de-force* fueled her vision of critical theory as an alternative to the "rigid, scientific pretensions"[43] of structuralism and Russian formalism.

In the late sixties *Tel* Quel became the intellectual stronghold of the younger generation of post-structuralist theorists in France. Its contributors, from Barthes, Foucault, and Derrida to Genette, Todorov and Kristeva, introduced a new concept of "history as text..and of writing *(Ecriture)* as *production,* not representation" (Moi, 4). History, literature, and even politics could then be considered as texts in progress, threads of discourse that suggest possible perspectives, rather than determine final products.

Later involvement in the political Left leaves Kristeva cynical about politics as a medium for reform. In the 1980's she argues for the need to elaborate a more complex understanding of the non-political aspects of human life. It is this distancing from political activism, as well as a disappointing encounter with the feminist movement in France, that inspires Kristeva to embrace psychoanalysis as a more authentic resolution of absolute meaning on the one hand, and the collapse of meaning, on the other:

> The psychonanalytic interpretation, then, is precisely one that is poised in the space Between One Meaning and the deconstructive, rejection of all truth...[44]

---
43 Toril Moi, ed. The Kristeva Reader. New York, Columbia University Press, 1986, p. 2.
44 Ibid., p. 15.

Psychoanalysis is the place where the science of the "mother-child dependence" (Kristeva, Les Cahiers du GRIF, 32, p. 23) and the "imaginary of the work of art" (p. 23) collude to produce a "subject-in-process in the symbolic order" (Moi, p. 15). There is no signification without a collaborative, open-ended effort between imagination and theory, art and science.

Although recently identified with psychoanalysis and its discourse, Kristeva's thought underwent a series of transformations that cross, and at times blur, the boundaries of disciplines. Critic Alice Jardine proposes three distinct Kristevas:

> "...the Kristeva of the '60s, who develops the new science semanalysis; the Kristeva of the '70s, who tries to describe a subject that has been repressed in Western history within the limits of totalitarianism and delirium; and the Kristeva of the '80s, who explores the deep logics of psychic phenomenon." [45]

Yet whether her chosen medium is linguistics, politics, literature or psychoanalysis, the dialectic she exposes is the same: the creative compromise between subject and other, identity and difference, which avoids "both the totalitarianism of *absolute identity* and the delirium of

---

[45] Oliver argues that there is even a fourth Kristeva of the '90s, who reverts to psychoanalysis and fiction as a forum for political debate. (Kelly Oliver. Reading Kristeva. Indiana University Press. 1993, p. 14).

complete negation... (italics mine) "(Oliver, 14). For Kristeva, ultimate truth is one that is not absolute, simply because it listens to the unsettling truth of alterity (difference or otherness), which by definition can never be subsumed by the principles of reason or identity. The irony of her theory of the absolute is that in de-absolutizing the traditional notion of transcendence, she discovers a truth that is all the more absolute, in that it restores the totality of the self and its relation to negativity.

The Kristevan notion of absolute truth departs from Gnostic models of rationalism which are rooted in the antinomies of mind-body, subject-object, reason-reality, sacred-profane. Kristeva's epistemology dismisses these as false dichotomies dictated by an outdated, reductive metaphysics that misconstrues the polyvalent relationship between the human psyche and the other.[46] How does Kristeva theorize this complementarity between self and other, between subject and transcendence, without one element of the pair collapsing into the other? Likewise, how does she avoid a stultifying oscillation that precludes any progress toward signification? For if the self were to cede to its negative impulses and give free reign to drive energy, meaningful discourse would be pre-empted: on the other hand if the subject is to have an

---

46 Kristeva refers to the notion of "other" as "alterity" - the fundamental condition of alienation that confronts the subject as he/she makes sense out of the Symbolic order or the realm of the Law – and a radically "other" unconscious to which he/she responds with ambivalence, horror, and fascination.

authentic identity it cannot submit to the overriding categories of the Absolute as ultimate ground of truth - whether it be a deity, a transcendental signifier, or the ethical prescriptions of the ego/superego complex. Kristeva's unique model of human subjectivity and truth is one that brackets the logical and ontological dichotomies of Western metaphysics. The subject is never fixed, always in transition, transforming itself according to the dialectically related structures of the "semiotic" and the "symbolic."[47]

Neither the logocentric Absolute of Western Metaphysics, nor the anarchic negativity of revolutionary art meets the demands of Kristeva's neo-theoretical construct; yet she is determined not to revert to a nihilistic rejection of metaphysics. Her evolving body of work can be seen as an ongoing attempt to mediate the paradoxical need for a meaningful transcendence that nevertheless upholds the free play of negativity inherent in language and the formation of psychic freedom. As Kelly Oliver explains in "Reading Kristeva",

> .....the problem is traversing the fine line between complete anarchy and totalitarianism; a complete overthrow of the Symbolic (the domain of the Absolute) would be anarchy. It would be abolition of human life. On the other hand, a complete repression of the semiotic leads to the tyranny of Symbolic law.

---

[47] The autocratic, pre-oedipal body is what Kristeva labels the "semiotic". Kristeva refers to it as "...the place of heterogeneity of sense." Kristeva, "Le Sujet en Proces" Polylogue. Paris, Seuil, 1977. The "symbolic" realm is the "always split unification of the signifier and signified....it allows the subject to engage in the process of signification." Kristeva, Revolution in Poetic Language. Trans. Margaret Waller. New York, Columbia University Press, 1984, p. 49.

Kristeva wants to avoid both of these extremes.[48]

---
[48] Oliver, p. 11.

What is unique to Kristeva and marks a progressive move in contemporary psychoanalysis is not so much her portrait of an Absolute that is unnamable, beyond the bounds of reason and by definition irresolvable (ab-solute); modern criticism and philosophy had already relinquished all claims to defining the Absolute. It is, rather, her revolutionary epistemology that completely redefines the nature of human identity and its relationship with the Absolute. The body, replete with drive energy and its forces of destruction, is not divorced from the rational mind and its more ennobling quest for knowedge and truth; mind and body, reason and instinct, are mutually defined and co-dependent. Rather than the gnostic dualism which pits both at odds with each other in a frustrated quest for mastery, Kristeva's epistemological paradigm recognizes an element of otherness in each pole, resulting in a dynamic conglomerate where difference and play redirect extremes that are traditionally exclusive of each other. Rather than a body that is alienated from the mind in a struggle to assert itself in the rational, ego-dominated world of the Symbolic, Kristeva's body nurtures a semiotic *chora* that is always and already inscribed with archaic traces of language and the realm of the symbolic. Likewise, judgments and propositions, concepts and

---

.

theories, these functions of the symbolic are not devoid of some liminal, (Kelly, 36) corporeal foundation - traces and signifying marks that revert it back to the primitive beginnings of the subject's formation:

> ...the heterogeneous flow...already dwells in a human animal that has been highly altered....Significance is indeed inherent in the human body.[49]

Ultimate Meaning, Truth, and Being do not dwell within the confines of reason; meaning is prefigured and its shadowy traces present in the body's first tentative impulses to separate itself from the undifferentiated bliss of the mother-child dyad, "....the power of semiotic rhythms....convey an intense presence of meaning in a presubject still incapable of signification. "[50] Likewise, once the subject has crossed the "thetic" threshold, [51] it has not left the body behind: the semiotic is never completely repressed, but makes itself heard as the voice of difference and alterity in a world of sameness and conformity.

Yet if body and mind, nature and culture, existence and essence have been polarized since the beginning of Western thought, how does Kristeva propose to reconstruct their interaction and avoid the pitfalls of metaphysics? The Kristevan paradigm establishes a place for the Absolute - an unnamable transcendence - but rather than relegate it outside the realm of human

---
[49] Kristeva, Powers of Horror. New York: Columbia University Press, 1982, p. 10.
[50] Kristeva, Tales of Love. New York, 1987, p. 62.
[51] Oliver, p. 40.

thought where it has traditionally resided, it is now the ligament that binds the subject and the other. Furthermore, the Absolute sheds its phallic, almighty character and assumes the carnal attributes of the maternal body. Maternity, for Kristeva, is a bridge between nature and culture, the drives and the Symbolic order. The mother's body is the "pivot of sociality, at once the guarantee and a threat to its stability.[52] As the first configuration of alterity in the subject's coming to be, the Mother holds the allure of a metaphysical ame of the Father, the fascination of the sacred, but because the maternal has no independent existence except in symbiosis with the child, it is an Absolute that obtains its identity through mutual inter- dependence with the subject:

> This (maternal) other is not yet autonomous; it depends on the subject. As such, it threatens the "almightiness" of the Symbolic, which requires an autonomous and inaccessible Other.[53]

In a radical move away from the Western glorification of the rational Absolute, Kristeva brings the seminal importance of the maternal body to the forefront of signification. The subject's primitive, sensual relationship with it, and not with a stern, linguistic Father, opens a creative space that is the precondition for language, meaning and the formation of loving social bonds. The movement

---
52 Edith Kurweil, "An Interview with Julia Kristeva," Partisan Review 53, no. 2, 1986, p. 29.
53 Kelly Oliver, p. 67.

toward the Absolute is not an alienating quest for the approbation of an omniscient Other: the Absolute is an intimate part of the subject's struggle to reconcile bodily drives and the desire for meaning - to harmonize the semiotic and the symbolic.

Yet how can the Absolute be both transcendent and immanent? How can it be so radically other (unnamable) yet always and already a part of one's archaic, pre-symbolic being? By situating the Absolute in the body's early formative coming-to-being and by redefining the Absolute as a paradoxical 'transcendence from within,' Kristeva arrives at an unorthodox synthesis of self and other; hers is a paradigm for the resolution of contingent existence and absolute essence that philosophers from Plato to Heidegger theorized, but could never develop beyond pure speculation. The Kristevan Absolute is not a contrived coupling of mutually exclusive terms but a natural complementarily between two radically separate yet co-existant human tendencies: the semiotic, situated in the maternal psychic receptacle called the *chora,* and the symbolic impulse toward discourse, conceptualization, and judgment.

Kristeva lays the groundwork for this dialectical Absolute by re-examining and reconfiguring the traditional boundaries of inner and outer, unconscious and conscious, self and society. She finds emergent symbolic structures pre-existing in the evolving proto-subject as well as traces of bodily impulses present in the logic of the linguistic and social self - two modes of psychic expression that had been traditionally considered separate and discrete. For example, Kristeva analyzes the primitive relationship between the infant and its first contact with the not-self: the mother's breast as the ambivalent site of comfort and desire. At this primitive stage in the infant's formation, the breast cannot yet be grasped as an object apart from the child's bonding/sensory response to it - yet Kristeva maintains there is a pre-symbolic identification with the mother's breast that serves as the originating model for objectivity. The breast is not an object for the infant but a "model," a "pattern" (Kristeva, Tales of Love. New York: Columbia University Press, 1983), p. 25). Oliver argues that this early identification with a proto-object is "... intrasymbolic ...in a very primitive sense...It prefigures and sets in motion the logic of object identification in all object relations... "(Oliver, 72). Archaic patterning of liminal subject-object relations sets the stage in the body itself for what is later to become the I-Thou/Subject-Predicate landscape of the discursive Symbolic. Matter presages mind and this prefiguring, we shall see, is duplicated in the relationship between subject and Absolute.

Kristeva's paradigm departs from Rationalist ontology which gives epistemological priority to a transcendent, hypostatic Absolute: Reason. Reason exhibits itself in the eternal forms of mathematics and logic, nature echoes the perfection of the Divine mind, and the poet evokes the Ideas of Beauty and Truth. In the Kristevan Absolute, on the other hand, truth is neither reflected in the eternal Forms nor contemplated through the exercise of reason; it is an emerging, unfolding process of indefinite becoming. For Kristeva there can be no repose for the subject in its quest for absolute truth *(jouissance)* - for this would be none other than an endorsement of the alienation of self and other from which Western metaphysics could not escape. What is sought is an "objectality in the process of being established rather than in the *absolute* (italics mine) of the reference to the Phallus..."(Kristeva, Tales of Love, p.30).

In traditional Freudian and Lacanian psychoanalysis the Phallus represents the Law of the Father, the set of social constraints that determine ego formation. The subject undergoes a rite of passage from sensual immersion with the maternal body to language, thought and identity only because of the stern interference of paternal law. What permits the subject to enter into signification is the Father's word, the transcendental signifier, the symbolic, transcendent Other. Yet for Kristeva, the passage from the semiotic to the symbolic, from drive to signification is not dictated by the logic of the word alone. Equally as important as the logic of negativity and rejection of the mirror stage are the

> ...archaic stages preceding the mirror stage...This process can be called imaginary, but not in the specular sense of the word, because it passes through voice, taste, skin, and so on....[54]

This visceral, material imagination[55] preconditions the not-yet-subject to be receptive to the raw materials of signification. It is sensation, rhythm, touch, what Kristeva later calls the "musicality" of language, and not discursive language, that lay the syntactic and significant foundations for meaning.

The linchpin of Western metaphysics is the notion of an ultimate transcendence that cannot be conceptualized without mediation. Theology proposes a God who is "the Word and yet whose Name cannot be spoken"(Kristeva, Histoires d'amour, (Paris: Editions Denoel, 1983), p. 313). Philosophy posits a rational Essence that beckons the intellect with the specter of absolute truth, all the while declaring it to be beyond the scope of existence. Kristeva's secular transcendence retains the attributes of the Western Absolute with its "cult of the irrepresentable" (Kristeva, 313), but here the unyielding, tyrannical signifier--God the Father--is cloaked in the mysterious garb of a 'father-mother conglomerate'. Kristeva ousts the teleological thrust of metaphysics without debunking the centrality of transcendence. The fusion of paternal/maternal, symbolic/semiotic elements in the Kristevan absolute

---

54 L. Appignanesi, ed. "Julia Kristeva in Conversation with Rosalind Coward," Desire. London, ICA Documents, 1984, p. 22.
55 Later I will discuss Bachelard's "material imagination".

diffuses the supremacy of rationalism and revives the repressed materiality that Western thought had relegated to the status of the irrational. Revisited through the dynamic of psychoanalytic transference, this imaginary father provides a "sense of completion and wholeness that combines the maternal gratifications and the paternal prohibitions" (Kristeva, 29).

If the Absolute is no longer the throne of reason and language; if it comprises both the nurturing rapture of the maternal womb and the insurgent rejection of paternal Law, Kristeva must reinvent a discourse that is compatible with both. She does this by dispensing with rationalist, essentialist epistemology as the paradigm for theorizing the absolute. What is needed, instead, is an imaginary identification with the father-mother structure that fulfills the subject's desire for both maternal body and Symbolic order. Desire and language are inclusive in the Kristevan model of psychic development; it is no longer the stern Father who rescues the child from drowning in the "maternal container," but rather the imaginary father who helps the child re-acknowledge his debt to the "...rhythms, intonations, and echolalias of the mother-infant symbiosis..." (E. Baruch and L. Serrano, ed., "Interview with Julia Kristeva," Women Analyze Women, (New York: New York University Press, 1988), p. 157).

CHAPTER FOUR: ART OR SCIENCE?

Kristeva's later devotion to psychoanalysis as the space where the subject can confront the multiple sublations of the modern absolute marks a shift from her earlier focus on semiotics and the search for a rigorously scientific theory of signification. Yet Kristeva the semiotician and linguist whose project in the mid-seventies was to create a new science of *semanalysis* exhibits many of the central concerns of the psychoanalyst-to-be, though shrouded by different terminology. *Semanalysis,* she urges, should borrow the constructs of the exact sciences, but must attempt to articulate those aspects of language and theory that do not signify: tone, non-meaning, rhythm. There is an inherent intertextuality to every signifying field, such that for all signifying systems

> ...the place of enunciation and its denoted "object" are never single, complete [italics mine], and identical to themselves, but always plural, shattered....[56]

Science seeks the unicity of meaning - the formal integration of reason and reality.   Semiotics, as the "place where the sciences die..."(Kristeva, *Semeiotike. Recherches pour une Semanalyse,* 1968), p. 78), addresses what

---

[56] Appignanesi, p. 60.

cannot be accounted for by denotative language - the heterogeneous element that "...challenges the very possibility of science" (Oliver, 92).

Mary Midgely, philosopher of science and social critic, voices some of the same concerns as Kristeva in her diagnosis of the myth of "science as salvation".[57] Modern science, she finds, offers updated answers to the age-old metaphysical questions "what are we here for?", "what is man?" - questions to which mythology and religion had offered naïve explanations. Cosmologist Stephen Hawking likens the scientific endeavor to a quest for "...nothing less than a complete description of the universe we live in" (Hawking, 13). He even ventures to equate cosmology, the science of the origin and workings of the universe, with "the ultimate triumph of human reason... (akin to knowing) the mind of God" (Hawking, 175).

Physicist Paul Davies declares the goal of science as no less than total control of the universe. Man will declare himself "lord... of the universe"[61] when he has succeeded in manipulating space and time to fit the dimensions of hypothetical models that were hitherto unthinkable, and at best improbable.

---

[57] Mary Midgely, Science as Salvation: A Modern Myth and its Meaning. London, Routledge, 1994, p. 1.

This unshakeable faith in science's ability to predict and control the physical world is mythologized in the practice of "scientism", which Midgley defines as "the idea of salvation through science alone" (Midgley, 37)." Yet despite the megalomaniacal truth claims of scientism which persist in the practice of scientific realism, contemporary physics is marked by a "shifting from substance to relation..." The consideration of being as an emergent system of relations - no longer an irreducible particle that can be observed - debunks the very notion of substance and signals a death toll for orthodox metaphysics.

Kristeva's portrayal of the analytical dialogue as the seat of an imaginary, provisional construct of truth recalls the relational model of modern physics. A thoroughly modern science in which neither subjectivity nor objectivity are absolutes, psychoanalysis experiments clinically with the dialectical paradigm of physics. Neither analyst nor analysand exerts ultimate power over the therapeutic process; rather, the artistic scenarios composed by the analyst are modified by the analysand, who in turn suggests alternative models that are integrated into an imaginative play of proto-theories. Subject and object are no longer separate entities that can be "clearly distinguished" (Kristeva, La Revolution du langage poetique, Paris: Editions du Seuil, 1974), p. 362), such that an absolute pronouncement of meaning can be decreed.

Kristeva is clearly not advocating a return to Romanticism's anthropomorphic view of nature; she is a daughter of the post-Industrial West and endorses the objectivity of knowledge, whether it be that of the text or of psychoanalysis. What she is against is the uncritical acceptance of the "scientific attitude" - the absolutizing of the scope of scientific practice and its totalizing quest for a final theory. She is a staunch opponent of scientism and its attempt to coin a "universal language - a single, vast ordered pattern, mirroring the pattern of the universe and revealing all truths" (Midgley, 61). Bacon's hope that one day scientists would "conquer and subdue nature... (and) discover the secrets still locked in Nature's bosom" (Anderson, Fulton H., The Philosophy of Francis Bacon, 93) is as absolutist as the modern physicist's bold presumption that we can 'know the Mind of God'.

As we have discussed, Kristeva's early practice as a semiotician and linguist lay the foundation for her eventual embracing of science as a hermeneutical model. Despite her penchant for the artistic, her praise of fluid structures, her insistence on the undecidability of the *sujet en proces* (subject in process), and her early fascination with the carnivalesque literature of Bakhtin, Kristeva always lends at least equal credibility to the symbolic discourse of the text and its labyrinthian composition - i.e., its problematic relationship with the underlying drive-based structure that seeps into the text despite itself. Yet while she may admire science's quest for a unified explanatation of reality as noble if not ambitious, she is unmistakably intolerant of science's eclipsing of the semiotic, both in human nature and otherwise. She is categorically opposed to what Brian Easlea refers to as the "mechanical philosophy":

> ...a radical 'de-mothering' of nature and the earth in preparation for, and legitimation of, the technological appropriation of the natural world that the mechanical philosophers hoped they and their successors would undertake[58]

Instead, Kristeva sings the praises of the passionate tension between a sensual, infantile embracing of the maternal body, and a rational, 'symbolic' discourse that struggles to lend a voice to that body in her unorthodox narrative, *Stabat Mater.* It is in the very textual space of this unorthodox narrative that the scientificity of the symbolic, in stark contrast with the spontaneous utterances of the unconscious which has not yet crossed the *thetic* boundary, is structurally and semantically made present. The binary structure of the text, its striking juxtaposition of the 'sound' of the semiotic and the 'word' of the symbolic, is a hypostatization of a self that is never neatly divided and always in the process of questioning and creating meaning. For Kristeva, to reduce the subject to either the semiotic or the symbolic would be tantamount to a betrayal of the irreducible dynamic in which they are the forces.

---

58 Brian Easlea, Science and Sexual Oppression, p. 73.

Kristeva's preoccupation with a practice that emulates the rigor of scientific method and yet is less (or more) than a science" (1969, 78) sets the stage for her subsequent conversion to psychoanalysis as the meeting place of science and art. Psychoanalysis is, she discovers, able to indulge in the "other scene"[59] - that which lies outside meaning-yet in a meaningful way, remaining faithful to the objectives of scientific method. Like semanalysis, psychoanalysis looks to the body for the inception of meaning: it pulls back the "...veil of representation to find the material signifying process" (1974, 103). It sees discourse not as monolithic structure that dilutes meaning by reducing the word to its mimetic function, but rather as a fluid process that is punctuated by semiotic drive charges alternating with symbolic stasis.

Kristeva's educational background in linguistics and criticism lent a decidedly literary bent to her formative works in the 1960's and '70s; at this early stage, language-in particular, poetry--is seen as the privileged locus of the semiotic and symbolic, where "meaning is constituted but is then immediately exceeded by what seems outside of meaning: materiality" (Kristeva, <u>Revolution in Poetic Language,</u> trans. M. Waller, (New York: Columbia University Press, 1984), p. 100). The literature of the avant-garde is revolutionary in its ability to resurrect and discharge the drives that realism and

---

[59] Here she refers to Freud.

representation keep in check. For Kristeva, the residual non-sense that is left after the transcendental signifier has withdrawn its authority is none other than semiotic drive energy—the repressed maternal *chora* and its forgotten meaning[60]. For Kristeva this dynamic materiality exists in a state of co-dependence with the symbolic such that neither pole can function without the continued support of the other. Modern poetry announces a new language that can capture both the "pulverization of meaning" (1974, 102) that is the semiotic, and the "symbolic barrier" (1974, 102) that is the precondition for meaning. The passage through the symbolic ensures that drive energy does not fixate in "...an opaque and unconscious organicity" (102); yet the poetic negation of the semiotic prevents the oppressive rule of the Absolute. The lyricism of poetry, with its attention to rhythm, tone, play on words, rhyme, invokes the semiotic disposition that Western metaphysics cannot recuperate.

Avant-garde poetry is a revolutionary voice where meaning is both negated and restored. It negates any claims to a priori absolute truth by refusing to re-present metaphysical truth claims; and it restores by tapping into unfettered drive forces that contain meaning in its nascent form, before language and culture have begun to homogenize it. Aesthetics, then,

---

[60] Heidegger, too, speaks of the "forgotteness of Being", Heidegger, p. 134.

deconstructs the Western Absolute, exposes its ideology, and opens the possibility for a liberating transcendence that "kills, thinks and experiences *jouissance* all at the same time" (Kristeva, Desire in Language: a semiotic approach to literature and art. (Oxford: Blackwell/New York: Columbia, 1980), p. 206).

The poetic text is a recollection of the heterogeneous element that lies outside the bounds of reason, identity, and truth; this zone of negativity where the subject is constantly destabilized nevertheless can only take form in and through the Symbolic. Without the structure of language and thought and their prescribed categories of meaning, the semiotic would be "psychotic babble at best" (Oliver, 101).

How, then, can modern poetry remain true to its revolutionary calling if it must ultimately conform to the structural demands of the Symbolic? Kristeva argues that in its questioning of the ontological and semantic status of language itself, poetry revolts against the absolute authority of the Symbolic. By using language to turn on itself, art performs a sleight of hand that destabilizes the very foundations of culture; through the beauty of what she names "abject literature", art can name the repressed horror of society that the Western Absolute by definition cannot. Rather than rationalize the murderous, negative impulses that found our society by erecting institutions and ideologies that sublimate those irrational forces, Kristeva legitimizes an aesthetic that discharges semiotic violence in a cathartic release, in poetic form, where the subject can recall his destructive origin and revisit his pre-symbolic dimension without threatening the status quo. She writes, "Without master, this universe has rhythm; without Other, it is dance and music; without God, it has style..."[61] Freed from the dehumanizing effects of a repressive Absolute, the self can revel in its newfound freedom - a "dancing, singing, and poetic animality" (1984, 79).

Revolutionary poetry exhumes the semiotic, lending it an authentic voice through the Symbolic. If semiotics is a science of that process of revalorization- a science that does not merely reveal the truth of reality, but reflects on the dynamics of the process of knowing itself,—how does one explain Kristeva's need to turn to psychoanalysis? Have not poetry and semiotics offered the most authentic resolution of the dilemma of art and science? The answer lies in her conception of the couplet "semiotic/symbolic" and their irresolvable complementarity. The semiotic drive forces, while she seems to want to define them as "the voice of a raw corporeality" (Oliver, 105), are not heterogeneous to the realm of the symbolic, but an integral part of the process of signification which is itself heterogeneous. And if language is polyvalent, heterogeneous, made up of a composite of meaning and nonmeaning, then neither science

---
[61] Kristeva, Desire in Language, p. 179.

nor art suffice as meta-theories that define it exhaustively. What is needed is a critical language that is neither that of poetry nor that of science, but that oscillates between the two.

Psychoanalysis is at once a commitment to uncover the unrepresentable modern absolute, hence a quest for total knowledge *(scienzia),* and a secular profession of faith, an admission of failure. For the therapist to pronounce a final, comprehensive analysis of the psyche would be a reenactment of metaphysics. Kristeva distinguishes between the meaning and identity created in the space of the dialogue and the monolithic Absolute of metaphysics. It is never "One Meaning, The True Meaning... "[62] that the analyst tries to name:

> Psychoanalysis cuts through political illusions, fantasies and beliefs, to the extent that they consist in providing...an uncriticizable ultimate Meaning to human behaviour.[63]

The analyst is acutely aware of the impotence of discourse, the "incompleteness..of all language..." (Moi, 314). Yet this very denial of absolute meaning, for Kristeva, is what allows for the disclosure of a more authentic meaning "...within an essentially open interpretive process" (Moi, 311).

---

[62] Julia Kristeva, "Psychoanalysis and the Polis," Critical Inquiry 9, no. 1, September, 1982, in The Kristeva Reader, p. 314.
[63] Ibid., p. 304.

Whether it is the young Kristeva who extols poetry as the stronghold of revolutionary practice, or the later Kristeva who assigns to psychoanalysis the privileged role of meeting place between semiotic and symbolic, it is theory that remains the common thread that unites her work:

> Intellection-the logical explanation of the struggle between two heterogeneities--is the site of the most radical heterogeneity... (S)ubtle differences in rhythm or color, or differences made vocal or semantic in laughter and wordplay -keeps us on the surface of pleasure in a subtle and minute tension[64]

The subject reaches a state of ultimate wellness or psychic ecstasy, not by returning to the blissful womb of the chora , where rhythm, touch, and sound are the only ties to an "other", but by nurturing a tenuous balance between the desire for pleasurable fusion and the need to be a separate, knowing, judging identity. This tenuous equilibrium is arrived at through the hyper-vigilance of psychoanalytical discourse, which becomes the voice-- i.e., the theory--of the semiotic:

> ...analytic discourse is perhaps the only one capable of addressing this untenable place where our species resides, threatened by madness beneath the emptiness of heaven.[65]

---

64 Kristeva, 1974, pp. 179-180.
65 Kristeva, Pouvoirs de l'Horreur. Paris, Seuil, 1980, p. xi.

Psychoanalysis, at once a scientific method and an artistic discourse, is unique in its ability to unite theory and practice in that very state of *jouissance* which is the sign of the subject's release from the demagogy of the Symbolic.

How does Kristeva account for her radical shift from a faith in language as the *sine qua non* of a free human subject, to an allegiance to the science and practice of psychoanalysis? For Kristeva, psychoanalysis is a culmination of poetry; poetry speaks the drama of the subject's forgotten struggle to forge an identity by "abjecting"[66] himself from the maternal figure, but it can never free the subject from the soul-wrenching state of abjection. Art and religion are conduits for the cathartic release of the drives; but psychoanalysis alone is able to provide an "elaboration" (Kristeva, Black Sun, (New York: Columbia University Press, 1989), p. 24) of this process, both a positing of a theory that seeks knowledge or truth, and an implementation of a scientific *praxis* that aims at therapeutic change.

However seminal the role of the intellect for Kristeva, she is careful to maintain that the "knowledge effect" (1983, 276) achieved in psychoanalysis is that of a provisional construct. Analytic interpretation is far from "...the authoritarian domination of a Res externa, necessarily divine or deifiable" (1983, 276).

---

66 Abjection is not repression but exclusion of "unconscious contents." Kristeva, Powers of Horror, New York, 1982, p. 7. During the phase of abjection, the child begins to distinguish between dependence on the maternal body and independence from the maternal body. However, the "borders between....child and mother, nature and culture, subject and other...are called into question." Oliver, p. 4.

The truth that the analyst suggests is a work of the imagination that is "...much closer to narrative fiction than philosophical or scientific truth" (Kristeva, <u>In the Beginning Was Love: Psychoanalysis and Love.</u> (New York: Columbia University Press, 1988), p. 19). Analytic discourse does not purport to disclose an absolute meaning, for meaning itself is inextricably bound with non-meaning and difference. Yet, there is an alterity built in to the psyche that, for Kristeva, takes the place of an external absolute or deity. That radical "other" lodged within the self discloses the heterogeneous, irrepresentable scene of the drives. Through the endless concatenation of interpretations that emerge out of the dialogic play between analyst and analysand, psychoanalysis challenges the immutability of "received truths" (1987, 58) and creates "innovative capacities" (1983, 15) for new meaning. Kristeva speaks of the responsibility of the analyst to resist the temptation to deliver a final, absolute interpretation:

> To the extent that the analyst not only causes *truths* (italics mine) to emerge but also tries to alleviate the pains of John or Juliet, he is duty bound to help them in building their own proper space....Help them, then, to speak and write themselves in unstable, open, undecidable spaces....It is not a matter of filling John's "crisis" - his emptiness - with meaning, ... But to trigger a discourse where his own "emptiness" and her own "out-of-placeness" become essential elements, indispensable "characters" if you will, of a work in progress.[67]

---

67 Kristeva, <u>Histoires d'amour</u>. Paris, 1983, p. 380.

Kristeva's "open, undecidable spaces" out of which emerges the unfinished psychic text begs the question of what, if any, truth can be found. If anything goes in psychic development, then there can be no absolute meaning that guides the subject beyond the precarious relativism of the therapeutic *hic et nunc*. It is just this contingency, however, that Kristeva determines to be the hallmark of true human freedom as well as the prelude to a more genuine transcendence. Far from a nihilistic smokescreen, psychoanalysis is "...the modest if tenacious antidote to nihilism in its most courageously and insolently scientific and vitalist forms" (1987, 63). The analyst enjoins the analysand to search for meaning, but a heterogeneous meaning that is exchanged and endlessly renewed between the two subjects. In this way, the concept of an absolute transcendence, "single, total and totalitarian Meaning..."(1981, 319), is replaced by the notion of heterogeneous signification in process.

CHAPTER FIVE: GOD AND THE ABSOLUTE

Where religion once provided an oasis of eternal meaning and immutable truth, the death of God left a wasteland of psychic wounds. The resolution of Kristevan psychoanalysis is to replace the traditional deity with a secular construct that avoids the snares of theology while at the same time preserving its mechanism for idealization, its movement toward psychic fulfillment (i.e., salvation through forgiveness):

> ...any modem imprecation against Christianity...is an imprecation against forgiveness... [T]he solemnity of forgiveness - as it functions in theological tradition and as it is rehabilitated in aesthetic experience... - is inherent in the economy of psychic rebirth.[68]

The legacy of Christianity that must be left intact is the "...specific economy of imaginary discourses" (Oliver, 130) that allows for a subjectivity actively engaged in the dialectic between redemption and damnation, symbolic and semiotic. The formal, imaginary structures of Christianity are the blueprint for a more resolute, authentic relationship with the absolute. Rather than an omniscient God who judges and condemns, the subject, through the imaginary construct of the

---
[68] Kristeva, In the Beginning was Love: Psychoanalysis and Faith. Trans A. Goldhammer. New York, Columbia University Press, 1988, p. 190.

loving father, identifies with a nonjudgmental other who "allows (him) to be reborn" (1987, 205).

Though psychoanalysis provides a surrogate womb for the analysand, it does not masquerade as a lay religion. The analyst invents and redrafts stories that depict possible psychic scenarios, refusing to condone homogeneous meaning that would, once and for all, characterize the subject's relation to a transcendent other:

> ... (Analysis) has nothing in common with lay religion or the initiation rites of a sage. The analysand delves beyond childhood to discover the immemorial origins of his desires; in the course of his analysis he recreates his sense of time, alters his psychic economy, and increases his capacity for working through and sublimation, for understanding and play.[69]

The subject is free to construct his own life-story, drawing from his forgotten past while at the same time projecting toward a salvific imaginary absolute that does not coerce him into identification with it, but serves as a provisional link between meaning and nonmeaning.

Thus Kristeva is unable to endorse the objectives of either science or religion. Science seeks an inclusive, objective transcription of reality, dismissing as nonsense that which resists its theoretical constructs; religion promotes a

---

[69] Kristeva, Soleil Noir. Paris, Gallimard, 1987, p. 57.

"theological idealism" that betrays the semiotic, reaching instead for the "Symbolic uniqueness of a beyond" (1987, 100). The absolute as sacred retains the allure of mystery and spirituality that Kristeva believes the modern subject still craves; but the metaphysical categories of religious discourse itself are inadequate. Kristeva's revalorization of the sacred and her simultaneous rejection of theism are a summoning of a new language that might speak the new meaning of the Absolute. What must be preserved from religion is not its substantive ideology, but "...certain phantasmic and linguistic knots on which the power of the sacred is built" (RPL 268); i.e., traces of archaic images and the interplay of manifold layers of meanings that exploit the undecidability of meaning, yet still hold the fascination of a beyond. Psychoanalysis, even more so than art, imagines a discourse that could possibly "...take the place of ...religious discourse which is cracking...(Appignesi, 25)" The Kristevan Absolute is an "outside of language" (1987, 66), neither Reason nor God, but the maternal body whose absence the subject is still mourning. It is fragments of the pre-oedipal glimpsed in the symbolic through wordplay and echolalia, but which can never be completely reconstituted.

Psychoanalysis' theorizing of a "primal object..........an other of language" (1987, 66) may appear to be a recasting of the traditional metaphysical mold.

Kristeva insists, however, that this extralinguistic other is

> ...not necessarily setting up a preserve for metaphysics or theology. (It) corresponds to a psychic requirement that Western metaphysics and theory have had...the good luck and audacity to represent.[70]

By replacing God or Being with an "unnamable" that the psyche is necessarily drawn to, Kristeva maintains the subject-object postulate that she believes is intrinsic to Western culture; at the same time, she avoids the alienating effects of a metaphysical Absolute which cannot accomodate the irrational and the contingent. The Kristevan absolute is neither divine nor rational; rather, it is the re-positing of the maternal Thing that lies beyond the scope of representation, beyond the Symbolic. The semiotic chora, while unrepresentable, nurtures the subject with the promise of fulfillment, if only he continues to fill its void with a language that speaks its manifold truths.

---

70 Ibid., p. 66.

CHAPTER SIX : POLITICS AND TRANSCENDENCE

Although active in the Communist party prior to May '68 and privy to the Maoist affiliations of the *Tel Quel* group of which she was a member, Kristeva quickly came to the realization that the lofty aspirations of political theory rarely translated into practical politics. She does not spare politics the same judgment meted out to religion, science, and art. She finds that its ideology is homogenizing in its repression of libidinal forces in the name of "transcendent political ideals" (Appignesi, 25). Like theology's desacralized God, philosophy's theoretical trinity (Reason, Being and Truth), and literature's transcendental signifier, politics submits the process of human engagement in the "polis" to a monolithic Meaning. The process of forging meaningful social bonds is deferred to an overriding ideal or principle which totalizes meaning - i.e., "justice", "liberty" or service to a political manifesto like Fascism or Stalinism. The creative forces that give rise to political activism are the very same libidinal urges that poetry and psychoanalysis catalyze. But in the case of politics, this residual nonmeaning has no privileged channel; it is sublimated in the name of a body of ready-made truths that the political subject can adopt.

According to Kristeva, rather than invoke an absolute "system of truths" by establishing a political institution or "interpretive summa" (Kristeva, Le Langage, cet inconnu, (Paris: Editions du Seuil, 1981), p. 319), modern politics should expose and identify with the "...crisis of modern interpretive systems without smoothing it over... "(319), without denying that all forms of representation, including the political, always implicate an alter-element that cannot be represented. Once again, Kristeva is calling for a science of human activity that submits its own activity to constant scrutiny. The literature, science and politics that she envisions are infinitely self-critical: each seemingly stable interpretation or theory is subsequently de-stabilized, reflected upon, and re-integrated in the space of a new paradigm. This politics of difference circumvents totalitarianism by denying the possibility of a final, absolute representation.

The traditional goal of the Western polis is to regulate contractual bonds so as to facilitate a homogeneous society that is economically and socially productive: a utilitarian goal, Kristeva would acknowledge, but one that by its own logic suppresses the very motor of social progress, that is, difference.

> My reproach to some political discourses with which I am disillusioned is that they don't consider the individual as a value.... That's why I say that, of course, political struggles for people that are exploited will continue, but they will continue maybe better if the main concern remains the individuality and particularity of the person.[71]

---
[71] Appignanesi, p. 57.

The subject of political action, no less than the writer, philosopher, or analysand, ratifies his subjectivity ironically by forging his identity in light of the differences he sees in others. This process of self-formation that is under constant self-criticism vitiates any absolute theory of subjectivity. Psychoanalysis, more than politics, can help the individual embrace alterity without displacing the negativity that makes us 'strangers to ourselves'.

Kristeva's critique of politics ratifies the same dialectical absolute that was explored in her earlier works on semiotics and poetry, one that is more compatible with the modern exigencies of alterity, dynamic subjectivity, and materialism. Always the concern is the same: how can one negotiate a fruitful exchange between absolute theory on the one hand-unscrupulous rationalism that levels differences--and an irrational anarchy that degenerates into meaningless negativity? How can one acknowledge the virtues of each-theory and practice, identity and difference, reason and the body--without lapsing into relativistic indifference? One of Kristeva's critics, Jacqueline Rose, is particularly mindful of this dilemma and claims that Kristeva "...proceeds to fall, at various points throughout her work, into one or other side of the psychic dynamic which she herself describes" (Jacqueline Rose, "Julia Kristeva: take two," <u>Sexuality in the Field of Vision,</u> London: NLB/Verso, 1986), p. 151). I would suggest that if Kristeva is guilty of favoring one to the exclusion of the other, it is always in light of her premise that even the body is perceived through the veil of representation; there is no absolute, unmediated experience of the semiotic. In other words, Kristeva's admitted oscillating between identity and difference is always and already an alternating from within the larger scope of representation.

Yet, is this not tantamount to the essentialist absolute of metaphysics--the Symbolic-by which reason and language confine the semiotic to the unnamable? Kristeva even goes so far as to refer to the "human being as the symbolic being...as the being who lives in language and who is not reduced just to the womb and to reproduction" (Kristeva, Desire in Language, (New York: Columbia Press, 1980), pp. 143-44). At face value, this admission would seem like a return to the Absolute of logocentrism, yet the representation that Kristeva speaks about is not the language of rational truth propositions. What she privileges in language is its musicality, its ability to evoke the libidinal forces that erupt out of and in spite of representation - in a word, the imaginary. Psychoanalysis is an artful science: as literature, it 'acts out' the play of negativity, and as science, it provides a theoretical recasting of "...the process underlying signification" (1974, 233).

CHAPTER SEVEN: LANGUAGE AND THE ABSOLUTE

Kristeva's later writings take on a decidedly more clinical bent, both in their subject matter and in their style and tone; more and more she incorporates case studies and profiles of analysands in her texts. Yet to call this shift toward psychonalysis (science) and away from poetry (art) as the locus of the Absolute a final conversion is a naïve misreading of Kristeva's synthetic model of the Absolute. We have already maintained that the common denominator in Kristeva's works on semiotics, poetry, psychoanalysis, religion, and politics is the pivotal status of language; yet this 'symbolic' dimension, we have shown, is anything but the rational abstractions of logic and metaphysics. Language, in its attempts to name "the unnameable"[72] must in a sense negate itself, becoming estranged from itself. It must become, in effect, "a fire of tongues, an exit from representation" (Kristeva, Tales of Love, (New York: Columbia University Press, 1987), p. 253). Even in the therapeutic wordplay of psychoanalysis, the language of the clinical dialogue is imaginary, non-communicative, connotative. Through the semantic associations solicited through analysis, the 'other' side of language—the affective, impulse-driven unconscious—is discharged into signification.

---

[72] Kristeva, Psychoanalysis and the Polis, (Toril Moi, The Kristeva Reader, 1986, p. 310.)

The multi-layered, polysemic dimension of language, whether in the poetic text or in the psychoanalytic session, absolves it of both metaphysical and nihilistic excesses. For Kristeva there is no outside-of-language, no absolute, in the form of a deity, rational Being, or transcendental signifier. Yet there is room for meaning, one which celebrates the unlimited pairings of word and sound, utterance and meaning, while still mindful of the "guard rails" (RPL, 209) that prevent language from dissolving into nonsensical babble. Once the idol of the metaphysics of presence has been shattered, language is free to connect the semiotic impulses that disrupt the conscious realm with glimpses, however dissimulating, of "...the unnamable, the unrepresentable, the void" (Kristeva, "Un Nouveau type d'intellectuel: le dissident, *Tel Quel,* 74 (Winter, 1977), 300).

In the absence of a grounding metaphysical presence-- a "mysterious presence or origin...outside language" (Anna Smith, Julia Kristeva: Readings of Exile and Estrangement, (New York: St. Martin's Press, 1996), p. 15)–the modern subject is haunted by an obsession with the "unnamable" (Kristeva. Le texte du roman. (The Hague: Mouton, 1970), p. 104). Where classical man deferred the question of his contingency to an a priori "essence" fashioned by metaphysics, modern man mourns the death of God by apostrophizing the absence itself—trying to fill the void by the very act of naming it. The old categories of metaphysics prove inadequate, however, and Kristeva calls our attention to the need for a new lexicon and a new theory of 'conceptualizing without representation'.

According to Kristeva, modern man has been exiled from the house of God and the transcendent ideals that derive from it. Alienated from society, which no longer erects the metaphysical signposts that had mapped his identity, and threatened by his own psychic interior, which destabilizes the norm with its alterity and difference, man can only express his "unhomeliness"[73] by foretelling the truth of modernity as agonizingly a-theistic and immanent. The harsh reality of the new absolute - non-being, drive-based affectivity - while inconceivable in the categories of rationalist metaphysics, passes over into signification (i.e., the "thetic" boundary) through the conduit or "influx of the semiotic" (RPL, 62). Glimpses of the body, "flashes of the unnameable" (Kristeva, Tales, 234-5) tear at the symbolic, exploding the orthodox categories of meaning with visions of the sublime:

> Not at all short of but always with and through perception and words, *the sublime is a something else that expands us, overstrains us,* (italics mine) and causes us to be both here, as deject, and there, as others (sic) and sparkling.[74]

The Kristevan absolute as both "here" and "there", immanent and

---
73 "unheimlich" (< German, "uncanny"). Freud sometimes defines it as "what arouses dread and horror." Kristeva, Polylogue, p. 219.
74 Kristeva, Powers of Horror, p. 12.

transcendent, brackets the metaphysical dualities of subject/object, self/other, body/mind, without resorting to a facile synthesis of opposites.

How can this new language which Kristeva calls for, one which is neither purely that of literature nor of science, represent that which is by definition unrepresentable? Does not a naming of the sublime, whether in therapy or in poetry, belie the very nature of the sublime as that which is beyond knowledge and understanding? The answer lies in a proper interpretation of the epistemological status of the absolute, for Kristeva. It is both an engagement with an external object -thus scientific in the primitive sense of the word- and an experience of awe and fascination akin to a mystical encounter, thus artistic in the modern sense of the term. The absolute is not known exclusively through the theoretical models of science; nor is it elicited through the art of poetic imagination. It is glimpsed in and through sensation and language and never completely manifest. Only the palimpsest of word, memory, dream, imagination, and desire can produce that curative state of *jouissance—the* therapeutic goal of analysis.

While Kristeva's psychological materialism denies any determinate knowledge of a transcendent absolute, it does not condone the alternative of radical positivism or scientism. The language of psychoanalysis is always a provisional, interpretive dialogue which is privileged with occasional moments "when the real and the imaginary coincide, and when language appears as if a luminous body outside the subject" (Smith, 39). Indeed, the transcendence that lures us with its paradoxically "dazzling obscurity" (Smith, 30) is none other than the body[75], at once intimately connected to the subject and irresolvably estranged from him (i.e., both "here" and "there"). And the language that speaks its truth is not the language of phallocentrism that seeks absolute knowledge, but the voice of the imagination, evocative of complexity and alterity. What gives language its significative power to pluralize meaning is the influx of the semiotic in the maternal element, or what Kristeva calls the "mother tongue". The drives, which originate in the mother-child dyad, explode the boundaries of logic and syntax (the symbolic) and force them to convert the body's enigmatic meaning into language. Rather than suffer in abjection, the subject is 'fed' by language, experiencing the "joys of chewing, swallowing, nourishing" (Tales of Love, p. 26) himself with words.

By positing the notion of a mother-tongue and acknowledging its failure to exhaustively represent reality, Kristeva is introducing the idea of a material 'other' that both resides in the subject and transcends the limits of rational discourse. It is intimately linked to the psyche's original rootedness in the maternal body, yet so radically heterogeneous to the realm of symbolic discourse that it fascinates with its difference. Kristeva's model, unlike the platonic theory of concepts participating in eternal forms, of the particular being subsumed by the

---

[75] Kristeva writes that when a "plurality of signifiers aims at...being signified," it results in the "sentiment of the body." Kristeva, "The System and the Speaking Subject," The Tell-Tale Sign: A Survey of Semiotics. Netherlands, The Peter de Ridder Press, 1975.

universal, discounts the hierarchy of Being and becoming. The individual experience of the body is so fundamentally other that it can never be fully incorporated into an "idea". Theory can never make present the experience of the body and its ambivalent state of abjection; for, "...there is no source outside of language, no phallic mother or deity from which the semiotic and the mother-tongue arise. We remain exiles from inside the symbolic" (Smith, 48). Yet language, when infused with the traces of the body, is able to imaginatively transpose the semiotic over into the symbolic.

The body is that elusive 'other' that denotative language can never completely domesticate. Only by re-sensitizing language itself, by disengaging comfortable associations of word and thought, can we break with mimesis and reactivate the drives. The Kristeva of *Semeiotike:* Recherches pour une semanalyse credits poetic discourse with the ability to penetrate the immediate, denotative meaning of language; the poetic word is outside the "bars of rationality" *(Semeiotike,* 91) that screen the body from communicative language, that filter difference from signification. Poetic language unearths a verticality in the word *(Semeiotike,* 9), a movement toward an absolute that is impossible to conceive of in the framework of the symbolic, for it is "...exactly that which cannot be thought within the whole conceptual system that grounds the contemporary mindset" *(Semeiotike,* 24).

Kristeva's goal, then, is to turn language "upside down" (RPL 615) so that what were previously unchallenged codifying systems now become questioning textual practices that invite "plural and heterogeneous universes" *(Semeiotike,* 14). On the other hand, her task is to create a transformation from within language, recognizing the fact that, as speaking and thinking beings, we are conditioned by an infrastructure of logocentric signification. How, then, can there be a revolution from within language, one that both respects the limits of discourse and yet questions the very premises of those limits? How, in a word, can language critique itself if it must use language to debunk its own categories? Kristeva introduces a new vocabulary of negativity that "explodes and shatters" (RPL 15) discourse, that refuses to take shelter behind the "veil of representation" (RPL 103) of conventional language, that "bursts, pierces, deforms, reforms and transforms" (103). Instead, she erects a new edifice that would replace Derrida's 'mansion of presence' and Heidegger's 'house of Being'[76] - both of which are founded on a solid logocentrism and the fundamental separation of subject and object. It is this ontological dualism that Kristeva is contesting, continuing in the tradition of Derrida whose concepts of 'trace', 'hinge' and 'difference' introduce alterity and

---

76 Jacques Derrida. Of Grammatology. Baltimore: Johns Hopkins University Press, 1976, p. xii.

incompleteness into the very structure of Being itself (Derrida, Of Grammatology. (Baltimore: Johns Hopkins University Press, 1976), p. 68). Her new "signifying edifice" (RPL 69) challenges language's hubris and its insouciant pairing of subject and predicate, signifier and signified. In the absence of an "Absolute Ideal, the Logos" (Smith, 91), meaning is contingent upon the subject's coming to terms with the irony and discomfort of a foreigner dwelling within him: the strangeness of the affect-driven unconscious.

To the metaphysical presupposition that textual discourse is the work of a *deus ex machina,* Kristeva counters that the text is infinitely significant from within. Literary discourse is no longer representative of a transcendent reality that is at once its origin and *telos,* but a "descent into the most archaic stage of (the subject's) positing" (RPL 83). While Cartesian models of mind polarized subject and object as *res cogitans* and *res extensa,* Kristeva posits the ephemeral *chora* as that which is the precondition for the separation of self and other. Prior to the demarcation of subject and object, the *chora* is a proto-object which must be "apprehended without the senses by a sort of bastard reasoning" *(Timaeus,* trans, F. Cornford, RPL, 239).

Thus it is neither through sensory perception nor through conceptual theorizing—neither empiricism nor rationalism—that the receptacle of the *chora* is known. In a word, the "rhythmical space" (RPL, 83) of the *chora* is the originating site where drives and primary processes are articulated as "precursory signs" or "imprints" (RPL 25), the embryonic psychical marks of the subject-to-be. Kristeva's challenge, then, is to find a way of theorizing that which by definition lies outside the realm of representation; for once the *chora* is normalized by rational, syntactical categories of thought, its very essence as proto-symbolic is vitiated. The "pre-objectivity" (Husserl, Ideas: General Introduction to Pure Phenomenology. London: Allen and Unwin, 1931, 258ff.) of the archaic semiotic body precludes any propositions or judgments that would articulate it as an object to be known. The obscure heterogeneity of the semiotic *chora* is, in effect, Kristeva's stubborn unwillingness to admit the ontological 'participation' of the subject in an Absolute. Subjectivity, she maintains, is neither sustained nor defined by a transcendent Being, but rather emerges and refines itself out of the negativity that is its very nonbeing.

If rational, denotative language cannot adequately express the dynamic of the *chora*, what does Kristeva propose as an alternative construction of meaning? Since communicative language (Smith, 98) fails to capture the generative processes of the inchoate subject, only a language that repeats the rhythm of the *chora* can voice its materiality without degenerating into a meaningless echo of biological negativity. Such a language takes place at the juncture of poetry (the "music of letters" which Mallarmean poetics epitomized), and theory (the Freudian science of drives), art and science. It is a language infused with the regenerative energy of the semiotic. Poetic language, when it is enlightened by the science of psychoanalytic drive theory, enables the repressed memories of the maternal body—the "thing itself (that) always escapes" (Derrida, "Difference" in <u>Speech and Phenomena and Other Essays on Husserl's Theory of Signs.</u> Evanston: Northwestern University Press, 1973, 104)—to cross over the thetic[77] boundary into the symbolic where it can signify without censure.

The poetic word is privileged in its ability to reproduce lyrically the drive-based sound units that are the wellspring of the semiotic. In their unorthodox experimentation with elided syntax, word plays, alliteration, and image-associations, French poets such as Mallarme unlock the rhythmic sonority of the word, thus tapping into "another scene" (RPL 27) of signification. For Kristeva, there is a direct correspondence between the drive-based function of the semiotic and the connotative patterns and signifiers in poetry. The process of determining meaning is not complete until the questioning subject re-encounters the mother-tongue that he had abjected and accepts it as an estranged part of himself. The poetry of Mallarme defamiliarized the word as unit of meter and syntax by musicating language to a "pre-phonematic" or "phonetic" state much like the "babble of childhood" (RPL 221). Kristeva surpasses Mallarme by associating specific drives with individual consonant

---

[77] Smith defines "thetic" as the "effect of positing ..that acts to orientate the biological body articulated by the drives towards the body of language, articulated by signs." Anna Smith, <u>Julia Kristeva: Readings of Exile and Estrangement</u>. New York, 1996, p. 99.

and vowel articulations. Certain phonemes, in particular those that are labial, nasal, liquid, or explosive (RPL 123), recall the archaic sounds of the pre-subject still intimately bound with the maternal body, thus reactivating semantic associations that "...reclaim the topography of the body... "(RPL 222). Critics such as Anna Smith berate Kristeva for reverting to the very idealism she sought to dismantle: by asserting a one-to-one correspondence between poetic word, psychoanalytic theory and the drives, is she not - they chide—invoking a new form of metaphysics in the guise of materialism? The mystery of the Absolute is reduced to biology; the word becomes flesh in the mundanity of the drives.

Is Kristeva in fact mythologizing the drives, thereby establishing a metaphysics of the body? And is not the mysterious labyrinth of the *chora* simply a deviation of the Absolute from the rational to the material, from logic to libido? It would seem that the "real" as that which "cannot be fully symbolised...into language"(Smith, 109)–drives, energy cathexes, etc.--is the materialist's answer to the Absolute, a neoplatonic reinscribing of transcendence within the body. Yet Kristeva states quite clearly that, although the body persists as inwardly transcendent, literature and psychoanalysis defer this mysterious other to an "infinitisation of meaning" (RPL, 613). Kristeva notes that, with respect to the undecidability of the signifying process, "...not a single person, nor any linguistic, discursive or rhetorical unity can contain the infinity of the process" (615). The nature of the Kristevan absolute as a process of recursive meaning sets itself apart from the monolithic ideal of the metaphysics of presence.

Kristeva patterns her concept of signification as infinite process (as opposed to mimetic representation) after the mathematician Cantor and his "infinite set theory" (Smith, 111). Traditional set theory, by positing an external infinity, reprises the *idees recuees* of 19th century French rationalism. In Cantor's infinite set, however, there is no absolute other, no distinction between internal and external, for "..each part may be equal to the whole" (Smith, 111). For the Kristeva of Revolution in Poetic Language, the negativity of the semiotic, unleashed by the poetic text, is not disciplined by an absolute substance or immutable essence (RPL 379-83). She has been the target of critics, who find her portrayal of the absolute to be excessively aggressive and destructive (Smith, 113). The experience of *jouissance,* or ecstatic pleasure, that overcomes the subject as the unconscious is initiated into language is not the milky nourishment of the maternal body but a violent joy that revels in the stark, inexplicable place of non-being.

Kristeva does not endorse the orthodox lines drawn between subject and object, symbolic and real; for her, the two are never "clearly distinguished" *(Serniotike,* 181) for the very reason that pure negativity precludes the subject's positing of judgments or assertions. There is a fundamental doubt that undermines all discourse, since there subsists no external absolute as guarantor of meaning and truth. Absent an a priori absolute, the floodgates of negativity are opened and the psyche is faced with the "unbearable monstrosity" (Kristeva, RPL in Smith, 118) that is the semiotic. Yet if the maternal *chora,* font of the semiotic, is at once a source of joyful fulfillment and a site of devouring horror, how can poetic language find its voice? The text can never represent the plenitude of Being; it can never be the final word that speaks transcendence. But neither, she continues, is it a spiraling negativity that signifies total loss of subjectivity: the text is a tapestry of interwoven "threads" (RPL, 148), a "linguistic fabric" (228) whose texture defies any absolute pattern. The disruptive process of the text itself "refuses...this fixity" (RPL, 542-3) and shatters the illusions of monolithic identity. The Kristeva of Revolution is an advocate of the individual as an open system, constantly in revolt against structures of identity that endow him with a finite ego. There is no question of transcendence, absolute presence or ultimate meaning: Kristeva refuses the very linguistic categories of metaphysics, replacing them with concepts that ignite the plurality of meaning and the irrecuperable dialectic of self and other.

Following the disillusioning experience of her travels in China and her early fascination with negativity as an intoxicating death drive, Kristeva appears to reconsider notions of transcendence as a means of salvaging some vestige of the classical notions of identity and subjectivity. She attempts to mediate the classical dualities of matter/form, body/mind, while safeguarding the newly-privileged status of the body. Once estranged from the comfort zone of communicative language, the "primitive lightning bolts" of which Mallarme spoke challenge our comfortable notions of identity and put meaning 'on trial'. Here, the Absolute reappears, not as ultimate Being but as "...a vision, a shiver, an instant of time or of dream without time" (Kristeva, Tales, p. 234) This momentary "flash" (Tales, 234) where the rhythm of the *chora* confronts us with our own desperate finitude, is the closest approximation to a divine encounter for Kristeva. Paradoxically, it is in coming to terms with our own negativity, in and through the alterity of the body, and by lending voice to the semiotic that we experience an epiphanic encounter with the sublime.

CHAPTER EIGHT: THE ABSOLUTE AS SUBLIME

Ultimately, as we have proposed, Kristeva abandons the cradle of the chora for the "fire of tongues" that is literary discourse. *Stabat Mater* is a clear evocation of the text as the space which most closely approximates the experience of a divine encounter, transposed as *jouissance*. Revolution in Poetic Language singles out the chora as the place of "...a non-being which contains the system, which conditions the becoming-system of the process, at the same time that it threatens the subject..." (539). In *Stabat* Mater, on the other hand, the precedence of the chora as immanent source of inchoate meaning is questioned. Art becomes the form par excellence of a mystical experience which recalls the union with the maternal body, yet transcribes it into the signifying mode of semiotic discourse rather than unstructured negativity. Only a language which is fueled by the mother-tongue can deflect the aggressive negativity that threatens the integrity and identity of the subject. Only if we "hear in language....the gouged-out eye, the wound, the basic incompleteness that conditions the indefinite quest of signifying concatenations..."(Powers, 88-89) can we avoid the 'horror vacui' that is abjection.[78]

In Powers of Horror, Kristeva develops the notion of the literary text as a fleeting vision of the sublime. But it is not only literary language that discharges

---
78 Abjection is defined as a "state prior to signification, where there are destructive, self-seeking drives, but no symbolic system in firm enough position to repress or displace these drives into speech...(Smith, p. 150).

the bodily drives as "slippages"[79] of the Absolute; now, the imaginary discourse of the therapeutic session as a cathartic "rebirth with and against abjection" (Powers, 31) is the ephemeral meeting place of subject and sublime. The Absolute for Kristeva is not a transmission of eternal truth, any more than the meaning of the text is an authorial depiction of 'reality'. It is in and through the pilgrimage of analysis that the sublime is intuited as a shared discourse on the process of signification:

> The binary message (in psychoanalysis) thus effects a shift from the I of pleasure to the you of the addressee and to the impersonal one that is necessary for the establishment of a truly universal syntax.[80]

Kristeva's suggestion is unequivocal: the sublime is none other than a universal language, neither subject nor object, neither here nor there, neither "I" nor "you"; it is the product of a frustrated quest for identity emerging out of the imaginary dialogue between analyst and analysand. The absolute is language reinvigorated by the influx of the semiotic, neither retreating into the undifferentiated pleasure of the maternal body, nor renouncing the body in deference to metaphysics.

Notwithstanding her bias toward the literary and psychoanalytic texts as avenues to the sublime, Kristeva's work belies a Proustian predilection for the raw, unmediated experience of beauty as harbinger of the absolute:

---
79 Similar to Roland Barthes' "glissement du sens" – the receding of meaning in the absence of representation.
80 Kristeva, Powers of Horror, p. 196.

> When the starry sky, a vista of open seas or a stained glass window shedding purple beams fascinate me, there is a cluster of meaning, of colours, of words, of caresses, there are light touches, scents, sighs, cadences that arise, shroud me, carry me away, and sweep me *beyond the things that I see, hear, or think....(italics* mine)[81]

The epiphanic experience of beauty suggests possible meanings to be derived; the particular conjures the universal and not vice-versa. The sublime appears in blinks and flashes of correspondence and wonder, through the conduit of sensation. For Kristeva the profoundly sensual nature of existence is precisely that which carries the subject 'beyond nature' - "beyond the things that I see, hear, or think". The sublime, therefore, transcends the body as well as reason and thought; it is neither the semiotic nor the symbolic but an imbrication of the two.

Just as <u>Powers of Horror</u> had investigated the abject subject pining for the idealizations (i.e., absolutes) that would make sense out of the semiotic-symbolic dualism, <u>Tales of Love</u> proposes a loving Imaginary Father as a mediating alternative to the autarchic absolute of metaphysics. Religion, no longer a plausible ground of meaning for the modern subject, leaves language parched. The image of mystery and transcendence that had

---
[81] Ibid., p. 12.

empowered language before the "collapse" of Christianity is now replaced by a loving third party that is able to mitigate the estrangement and angst of the modern subject. This it does neither by a return to the autocratic reign of contemplative thought, nor by surrender to the allure of unbridled drive energy. Kristeva instead acknowledges mystery and transcendence as an "elsewhere" that transforms us without suppressing difference. We are "empty dilapidated castle(s)" (Powers, 186) that require the distancing of idealization as the "condition for the very existence of psychic space" (Tales, 31). This idealising structure does not house the Law of the Father but an Imaginary Other which already dwells in the subject as a "fold" of otherness and alterity (Smith, 166). Kristeva writes, "We are immediately within *parousia*" (roles: 39);[82] the dialectic between indeterminate matter and absolute loving Ideal can never be wholly rationalized or "dissected into discrete elements" (Smith, 167).

The Absolute of metaphysics absorbs difference and dissolves the body by assimilating them as epiphenomena of rational knowledge. The Kristevan absolute maintains its status as 'other', but as a transcendence that resides in the structure of the psyche itself. She hereby reconfigures the classical antinomies of subject and Other, individual and absolute, particular and universal. The loving Imaginary Father is an exterior someplace which beckons the questioning subject who is 'in the process' (en *proces)* of forming an

---
[82] < Gk "presence" or "arrival".

identity; but this 'elsewhere' retains none of the attributes of a despotic deity or self-determining logos. It is a point of externality that draws the psyche to regions of itself hitherto unexplored, to a no man's land within its own interiority. Philosophy's "ego cogito", Kristeva maintains, must undergo a pentecostal rebirth: the semiotic's "tongues of fire" transform the subject of metaphysics into *"ego affectus* est" (Smith, 167). No longer poised between a body and mind at odds with each other, but nourished by a non-erotic, divine love - *"agape"*[83]- the subject can relate affectively to the Imaginary Father and thereby experience an idealising transformation, from within.

Unlike the destructive negativity typified by the manic *eros* of Plato's *Phaedrus*, whereby love and passion are obstacles to rigorous contemplation of the Absolute, Kristeva's spiritual love surpasses thought and its accompanying "violent, erotic urge to mastery... "(Smith, 172). For Kristeva, rationalism, science, metaphysics, religion - all are symptomatic of the Nietzschean will-to-power that is the source of Western civilization's *mal du siècle*. Accepting the Absolute as the sine qua non of ego formation, endorsing cognition as the only purposive activity of consciousness, deferring psychic patterns to the prescriptive ordinances of the symbolic and the rational - all are symptomatic of the contemporary malaise that Kristeva diagnoses as "estrangement." What is to be sought, she proposes, is a model

---

[83] <Christianity: divine love; spontaneous altruistic love.

of subjectivity like that of an "open system...capable of innovation" (Appignanesi, 21), one which is perpetually destabilized and reconstituted by the imagination. Language cannot secure salvation for the subject; the Word cannot speak eternity for our shattered souls. In an apocalyptic conjuring of the demise of the Absolute, Kristeva's The Old Man and the Wolves dooms the comforting words of God the Father to be replaced by "foreign words... (that) play the part of the seraphim..., flocks of angels... (that help us) soar through secret skies" (Kristeva. Le Vieil Homme et les loups. Paris: Fayard, 1991, 166).

It is important to insist on the non-recuperative nature of the Kristevan absolute: the psyche is nourished neither by the promises of saving Grace nor by the political might of Reason. The glimpses of the sublime that enrapture it are set against a backdrop of separation, lingering anxiety, and emptiness. We are forever in touch with the estrangement from the maternal body that first encouraged us to seek solace in language. Ironically, we are most healthy when, through the language of poetry or the language of psychoanalysis, we 'play' with the trauma of our homelessness. For "...those who are racked by melancholia," Kristeva advises, "writing about it would have meaning only if writing sprang out of that very melancholia" (Kristeva. Black Sun: Depression and Melancholia. New York: Columbia University Press, 1989, 3). To cover the wound is to sink into the banality of the symbolic and the solace of metaphysics and theology; to expose the wound and to speak about our exile is to become an agent of renewed subjectivity. Where Reason and God were the pre-modern "moments of transformation" (Smith, 186) through which the subject acceded to transcendence, now the subject is able to originate his own meaningful transformation: by resurrecting drive energy, encountering the Imaginary Father, and enervating language so as to tell its story.

Despite the collapse of metaphysics, the sublime persists in the metaphor of the written word and in the metamorphosis of the analytic session. For Kristeva the illumination of Being (the Absolute) appears as an analogical connection among people, things, time and place, preserved in the elegant correspondences of the metaphor. By transforming the fleeting aesthetic moment into literary images that recall its connection to the psyche, the word becomes evocative of the sublime, a "...token of *some real thing* (italics mine) behind appearances" (Virginia Woolf. Moments of Being. Grafton: Hammersmith, 1989, 81):

> In the experience of imaginative writing, due to the constant passage between words and perceptions, one encounters the spectre of a bodily restructuring, of a revitalization which is extremely pleasurable (juissif) and which opens a space for the illusion of eternal life - the soul of madness...It allows the reader to recover his/her own memory, his/her own body, and that can be a truly revitalizing experience.[84]

---

84 Vassiliki Kolocotroni, "Julia Kristeva," Textual Practice 5, 1991, p. 165.

Likewise, for psychoanalysis there is no revelation of truth other than that of the on-going reciprocity of psyche and analyst, who together fashion a new language that takes the place of a First Cause. Through the "alchemy of the word" that is the psychoanalytic dialogue, the subject enters into a state of "mystical metamorphosis" (Kolocotroni), 165).

Be that as it may, what is to prevent the subject-in-process from inhabiting a series of metaphorical identifies, none of which culminate in a stable self? Absent an absolute transcendence that absolves us of our contingency and given the provisional nature of Kristevan idealisation, what is left for the psyche but language and its palliative delusions of meaning? The Absolute, for Kristeva, is the paradox of an external space from within. It is a font of liminal truth within the psyche, from which and toward which the art and science of psychoanalysis is directed.

PART II

GASTON BACHELARD

CHAPTER NINE: Science and Literature - *Animus* and *Anima*

Epistemologist, philosopher of science, and literary critic, Gaston Bachelard was born at Bar-sur-Aube in 1884. He spent his childhood in Champagne and after finishing high school worked as a postal employee from 1903,1913, after which he earned his *licence* in mathematics and science. In 1919, after four years of military service, he began teaching physics and chemistry in the high school of his hometown, where he remained until 1930. He began graduate work in philosophy at the age of 35, acquired his *licence* in 1920, and in 1927 received his doctorate of letters and became professor of philosophy at the University of Dijon. From 1940 to 1954 he served as chair of the faculty of philosophy of science at the University of Paris. In 1954 he was named professor emeritus, but continued to publish and lecture on a part-time basis. He received the *Grand Prix National* des *Lettres* in 1961, one year before his death on October 16, 1962.

According to Bachelard, cognition is the product of an exchange and interaction between reason and reality:

> ...the confrontation of an isolated, rational human mind
> with an indifferent and meaningless world...is [a] naïve
> [postulate]. Scientific hypotheses, and even scientific
> facts, do not present themselves passively to the patient investigator but are
> created by him.[85]

---
85 The Encyclopedia of Philosophy (New York: Macmillan Publishing Co, Inc. & The Free Press, 1972), vol. 1 and 2.

Theory and experiment are no longer discrete ontological fields, but two poles situated dialectically within an "applied rationalism".[86]

Just as Bachelard expounds the interdependence of reason and reality in experimental science, likewise he postulates the defining role of the mind in art. In the case of both science and poetry, the a priori presence of the imagination synthesizes subject and object into a third term - "...the *project*[95] - in which they are mutually defined.

Gaston Bachelard, though acutely aware of the chasm between literature and science, at times goes to great lengths to underscore the *rapprochement* between the two. For Bachelard, the recent postulates of modern science have effected a gradual eroding of classical science's goal of absolute knowledge and have succeeded in bringing science closer to the relative truth of avant-garde literature. Science cannot deliver an exhaustive account of the workings of nature, no more than art can reproduce the absolute meaning of lived experience.

Modern science and poetry, for Bachelard, operate in accordance with two faculties that are diametrically opposed: concept and image. The rational methods of science are guided by abstract concepts while the art of the literary text is held under the sway of imagination. Between them, he

---

86 Bachelard, Le Rationalisme appliqué, Paris, P.U.F, 1949.

declares, "...there is no possibility of synthesis. Nor indeed of filiation" (Bachelard. La Poetique de la reverie. (Paris: Presses Universitaires de France, 1960), pp. 45-47).

It is for this reason that Bachelard's works often frustrate critics' attempts to find in them an underlying unity. His literary studies on imagination and those on the epistemology of science alike seem to mock any claims to unification. He insists:

> ...images and concepts are formed at opposite poles of mental activity: imagination and reason. A polarity of exclusion plays between them, in a way utterly unlike that of magnetic poles. In this case, the opposite poles do not attract, but repel. If one loves concepts and images, the masculine and feminine poles of the psyche, one must love mental powers with two different loves.[87]

As two distinct mental faculties that address disparate phenomena, reason and imagination require intellectual acrobatics to satisfy the exigencies of each. Rather than attempt to harmonize the two in a hybrid "imaginary science" akin to Kristevan psychoanalysis, Bachelard insists on their mutual exclusivity:

> When the concept assumes its essential activity, when it functions in a field of concepts, the use of images would ...weaken or even feminize it....The image cannot give matter to the concept; the concept, by giving stability to the image, would stifle its existence.[88]

---
[87] Bachelard, 1960, pp. 45-47.
[88] Ibid., pp. 45-47.

For Kristeva, the feminine chora, the foundation of the imagination, is nevertheless always and already marked with the traces of pre-symbolic functioning. And the masculine symbolic, the domain of reason and concept, erupts with the resurfacing of the semiotic body. The language of psychoanalysis, which is none other than an imaginary text, sets to work on the unraveling of this imbrication of reason and imagination. Bachelard is reluctant to define the two activities in terms of each other; image and concept, intuition and science are dichotomous aspects of man's essentially dual nature. It is in light of this polarity that any presumptions of "unitary approaches" (Tiles, 54) to absolute knowledge are flawed.

CHAPTER TEN: THE EPISTEMOLOGY OF THE ABSOLUTE

Bachelard condemns modern philosophy - i.e., metaphysics - for not allowing its fundamental tenets to evolve in tandem with the progressive, revolutionary transformations of modern physics. Because of this inability to adapt to the radical discoveries of contemporary science, philosophy languishes in its assertion of a knowable absolute and of rationalism as the sole epistemological method commensurate with it. It is up to philosophy of science to expose metaphysics for the illusion that it is, thereby enabling philosophy to adhere properly to the principles of contemporary physics.

When Bachelard states that "[science] in fact creates philosophy" (Bachelard. Le Nouvel Esprit scientifique. Paris: Presses Universitaires de France, 1978 (Paris: Alcan, 1934), 7) he is not forecasting the demise of philosophy, but merely suggesting that philosophy let go of traditional metaphysical presuppositions that ossify it with dated rational categories. Cartesian epistemology, heir to platonic Idealism, is founded on the deductive principle of reason and its cognitive process; reason acts as an "external standard" (Tiles, 26) by which all truth propositions are guaranteed. It is this absolute, rational arbiter to which metaphysics clings naively, while science has long since relinquished any claims to immutable, objective truth. Descartes' a priori intuition of space and extension and his acceptance of unquestionably 'clear and distinct' ideas justify the self-evidence of such empirical concepts as 'point', 'line', and 'plane'. Relativity theory, on the other hand, counters these claims with the principle of interrelations among concepts that are derived from a theoretical framework. Science lays no claims to self-evident truths; for, as Bachelard observes, "(it) is necessary to form reason in the same manner as it is necessary to form experience" (Nouvel Esprit scienfifiaue, 176). The Enlightenment quest for absolutely certain principles must give way to a more modest yet equally noble search for a provisional, approximate knowledge.

The epistemological correspondence that Descartes presumes exists between the observing subject and the perceived object is refuted by modern science, which denies any immediate 'given' in sensory perception. Quantum mechanics has already undermined the realism of particle physics; not only is sensation mediated by technical instruments, resulting in a subsequent alteration of the known object, but each investigation of a substance bears the interpretive imprint of the reigning theoretical mindset. Even at the quantifiable level the scientist never presumes that his experimental results are "in any way absolute and beyond further correction or refinement" (Tiles, 59). Both method and theory, then, determine knowledge and make absolute objectivity meaningless (NES, 177-80). Bachelard labels the

Popperian assumption of an independent material reality *"chosiste"* (NES, 42) and redefines the notion of objective scientific knowledge as progress tending toward objectivity rather than knowledge of absolute truth:

> The purity of a substance is thus the work of man. It should not be taken for something given in nature. It retains the essential relativity of human works.[89]

In a very fundamental way, then, Bachelard's recasting of scientific objectivity as an interrelationship between knowing subject and "functional" object, recalls the dialectical interplay of the Kristevan psychoanalytic dynamic, in which both science and art, reason and imagination pair in unpredictable patterns that yield no finished absolute, only a truth in progress.

Immediate, intuitive cognition, Bachelard believes, is a relic of classical realism which must be discarded. Both empiricism, which grounds knowledge in immediate sensory perception, and rationalism, which looks to a divine essence as the guarantor of an objective, rational order, are flawed. Both are the source of epistemological obstacles that preclude a more accurate, scientific way of accounting for objective knowledge. Nevertheless, Bachelard is adamant that intuitive, subjective knowledge plays an indispensable role in the pursuit of scientific objectivity. Absolute objectivity is never registered by

---

[89] Bachelard, Le Materialisme rationnel. Paris, 1953, pp. 79-80.

an impartial knowing observer; truth is derived from the reciprocal interaction between intuitive and discursive, or rational, modes of knowing.

Kristeva's notions of subject-in-process and semiotic-symbolic interplay fueled her concept of relative truth emerging out of the dialectical cooperation of art and science (both in literature and in therapy). Here, too, we see a rejection of an epistemological 'absolute' and its concomitant metaphysical presuppositions. Contemporary science, grounded in non-Euclidean mathematics, no longer looks to intuitive or perceptual foundations to objective knowledge; scientific truth ceases to be representational and is governed by abstract, rational constructs of a purely functional nature. Mathematics, by abstracting concepts "...methodically from the intuition which proposed them to us" (Bachelard. <u>Essai sur la connaissance approchee.</u> Paris: J.Vrin, 1973 (Paris: J.Vrin, 1938), p. 169), formalizes the content of experience by "...substitut(ing) totally the constructed for the given... "(CA, 174). The ontological status of mathematical objects is relational and corresponds to no independently existing reality.

Scientific truth, then, exhibits a radical departure from the realist, substantialist epistemologies of Aristotelian and Cartesian metaphysics. Its constructs, of a purely formal nature, have no ontological referent apart from their position within a coherent, rational system[90]. How, then, can there be any empirical, cumulative progress in science without an absolute standard by which to determine its objectivity? For Bachelard, objectivity is a palimpsest of successive approximations, each of which rectifies those that precede; it is possible only "...if one has first broken with the immediate object..."(Bachelard, La Psychanalyse du feu, (Paris: Collections Idees, 1949; Paris: Gallimard, 1938), p. 1). Knowledge is not catalogued inductively, but constructed according to the increasingly precise rectifications of scientific theories:

> Approximation is unachieved objectivation, but it is prudent, fertile objectivation, which is truly rational because it is at once conscious of its insufficiency and of its progress.[91]

The language of science – mathematics - utters no absolute truth about the way reality 'is' objectively. Its constructs, entirely conventional, offer so many rational frameworks which, when interrelated, form diverse theoretical perspectives on what constitutes objective knowledge. Without an ultimate standard of truth (absolute) or "neutral observational base" (Tiles, 116) subject

---
[90] Bachelard, Essai sur la connaissance approchee, Paris, 1973, p. 231.
[91] Ibid., p. 300.

to which evolving theories are judged, not only the notion of objectivity but reality itself must be redefined[92].

Just as Bachelard recognizes the constructivist nature of contemporary mathematics, so too he acknowledges the relativity of science and its progress toward objective knowledge. Before even initiating an investigation of a problem, scientists must "...develop a sort of topology of the problematic" (Bachelard. Le Rationalisme applique, (Paris: P.U.F., 1975; Paris: P.U.F. 1949), p. 56). It is not simply a question of positing theories that conform to observed facts, but of determining what justifies the inquiry in the first place, and then articulating a prototypical solution. Progress is on ongoing conversation between reason and experience, a dynamic exchange between theoretical and empirical considerations of the object of study.

Once more Bachelard begs the question of what, if any, reality can be known if modern science rejects both idealism and realism as categories of possible experience. If science is not to lapse into solipsistic speculation, the traditional notions of 'objectivity', 'physical reality', and 'knowledge' must be revised, if not revoked. Bachelard's analysis of approximate truth as an indefinite sequence of modifications that always falls short of absolute

---

[92] Science itself is socially and historically conditioned, since it develops along with changes in mathematics. Bachelard, Le Nouvel Esprit scientifique, Paris, 1978, p. 43.

knowledge recalls the infamous "thing-in-itself", a transcendent reality that eludes conceptualization. By admittedly committing itself to failure and eternally deferring a final theory of truth, science in effect reintroduces the very metaphysics that it set out to eradicate. Yet Bachelard avoids the spectre of a metaphysical absolute by insisting on the objective reality of an "unattainable limit" (Tiles, 129). This absolute, irreducible 'other' transcends the mind's ability to conceptualize it and remains resistant to the subject's cognitive will-to-power. The nature of the physical world is such that it is "...from the start posited as something of which our knowledge is, and must be, incomplete" (130). The assurance in mathematics that abstract formal constructs actually do reflect mathematical reality is absent in empirical science; for here objectivity is obscured by the irreducibility of the object being investigated and by the empirical conditions under which it is being observed. Because of the tentative accuracy of instruments and their resultant data, one can never assume an "absolute ...identity" (Tiles, 134) among phenomena. Quantum physics extends the jurisdiction of this uncertainty principle to the micro-physical level by substituting probability for precise measurement when it comes to observing quanta. Thus the object as an independently existing, discernible reality is no longer an unquestioned assumption. A 'probable' object is realized through progressively detailed measurements that alter the very nature of that which is observed.

CHAPTER ELEVEN: ABSOLUTE OF APPROXIMATION

Far from presuming that scientific theory conforms to the real world and yields absolute knowledge of it, Bachelard contends that modem science humbles itself in the face of an increasingly resistant reality. Yet, the parameter of failure ("insufficiency" (CA, 300)) and the constructive role of error in Bachelard's theory of approximate knowledge do not preclude objectivity; they merely reinstate the primacy of metaphysics in determining what objectivity is:

> The idea that objectivity is not given, but has to be attained, and the idea that there can be no disinfected, metaphysics-free science, are thus intimately connected. Science cannot do without metaphysics any more than it can do without induction, for the metaphysical framework is that which determines the identity of the objects we believe in.[93]

A fundamental belief in a theoretical macrostructure, validated by empirically verifiable laws, is ultimately what makes sense of phenomena. The objects of scientific study turn out to be none other than participants in an imposed rational order. In addition, these rational paradigms that generate objective reality are not the capricious imaginings of individual minds working in isolation. Bachelard underscores the inherently social nature of scientific objectivity, which relies increasingly on "intersubjectively agreed...classificatory scheme[s] (Tiles, 140)... that legitimize scientific practice. The laws that govern a particular scientific paradigm are ratified by a congregation of scientific 'believers'; and it is this system of

---
[93] Tiles, p. 138.

accredited concepts that in turn predetermine what future empirical criteria will be applied to experience.

Yet "mere intersubjectivity" (Tiles, 148) for Bachelard can never be the sole criterion for scientific objectivity. While it may seem that Bachelard condones the socio-historical validation of scientific theories, he is not in fact advocating a brand of "corporate, socialised idealism" (152) in which objective reality is filtered by concepts. It is not by virtue of a theory's acceptance by the scientific community that it is rationally justifiable; a theory contributes to objective knowledge not because it provides "factually objective statements....(about) self-subsistent objects" (153), but rather because it verifies a formal reality. Science does not mimic "...a world to be described. It corresponds to a world to be constructed... "(Bachelard, L'Activite rationaliste de la physique contemporaine, (Union Gonerale d'Editions, 1977; Paris: P.U.F., 1951), p. 65).

The Bachelardian absolute, seen in this light, is less a substantive transcendence than a hypothetical postulate of statistical probability - an absolute stripped of its ontological stature. Scientists operating within a particular historical continuum add progressively to a series of approximations, which gradually converge towards an ideal, postulated "limit" (Tiles, 156).

Language itself, whether that of ordinary discourse or of science, is equally incapable of exhaustively representing reality; for words and concepts are encrusted with historical and cultural "accretions" (Tiles, 158) which obstruct purely denotative signification. This limitation, for Bachelard, does not impede knowledge, but provides the impetus for dynamic inquiry which propels the rational mind forward to super-rational thought. The scientist, like the poet, is conditioned by the linguistic and discursive givens that are the inevitable starting points of creativity.

In La Philosophie du non, Bachelard traces the historical evolution of the concept of 'mass' in order to exemplify his theory of scientific progress as an incremental sequence toward to an unapproachable limit. If one refers to the pre-scientific notion of objectivity, mass "has a high degree of substantial reality..." (Bachelard, La Philosophie du non: Essai d'une philosophie du nouvel esprit scientifique, (Paris: P.U.F., 1975: P.U.F. 1940), p. 22)" and is in harmony with the anthropomorphic paradigm that Baconian science presupposed. As empirical science became more sophisticated, 'mass' became an operational concept which was defined by "quantitatively precise" (Tiles, 161) determinations of measurement. This treatment of mass as an "instrumentally determined" (162) concept reflected the uncritical assumptions of positivism - the most common of which was the idea that mass is a numerical quantity which resides in objects apart from the methodology of measurement. With the advent of Newtonian physics, mass was no longer defined as an objective, empirical given, but rather stood in relation to the conceptual apparatus bound by the laws of science. The notion of mass became problematic - neither directly observable by the senses nor immediately accessible to rational theory. Relativity theory problematized the category of mass even further: mass was "no longer treated as an invariant or essential characteristic of an object" (Tiles, 163). It came to be defined not as a substantial attribute of objects but as an open concept, defined "functionally" (163), as Bachelard puts it, by its relation to velocity. Finally, quantum mechanics continued the modern rejection of the absolute nature of mass by considering the possibility of negative mass, one which marks a radical departure from the objectual realism of both Baconian science and common sense.

CHAPTER TWELVE: ABSOLUTE AS DYNAMIC PROCESS

Bachelard's characterization of the epistemological revolution in modem science's conception of truth is best summed up in his paradoxical statement: "It is at the point when a concept changes its sense that it has the most sense" (NES, 56). This declaration, both perplexing and provocative, invites its audience to entertain the juxtaposition of two seemingly incompatible notions: truth and change. Scientific thought, Bachelard claims, is propelled dynamically by the process of "…repeated attempts at conceptualization…" (Tiles, 181) which revise concepts indefinitely. Whereas Cartesian epistemology is essentialist in nature—its rationale for truth claims is based on reference to a fixed set of "…indubitable, intuitively recognised truths" (181)—non-Baconian science questions and destabilizes theories that were presumed to be immutable and absolute. Yet, it is not only the intuitive truths of reason in the tradition of Aristotelian and Kantian metaphysics that must be demoted; the immediate intuitions of experience, i.e., experiment, are likewise subject to revision. Progress towards objectivity entails "questioning the unquestionable" (182), not as an intellectual afterthought but as an integral part of cognition. The possibility of an objective, absolute vantage point of cognition has been dismissed, as there is always the goal of an increasingly precise yet more abstract theoretical framework to come. The orthodox, rationalist-realist dreams of perfect correspondence between representation and reality give way to a more modest yet equally ambitious goal of "better approximation" (Tiles, 183).

Bachelard's characterization of modern scientific research owes much to the Kantian definition of reality as knowable to the extent that it constitutes 'possible experience'. The scientific unknown, like the celebrated "thing-in-itself", is considered outside the realm of knowledge by virtue of its being posited against the context of a "problematic" (Bachelard, <u>Rationalisme applique)"</u> - an epistemological model that provides a "schematic account...of what it would be to have objective knowledge..."(Tiles, 183). Against this backdrop of Kantian idealism, Bachelard introduces his own theory of cognition which, although idealist in form, rejects one of the most fundamental tenets of Kantian epistemology: the assurance that rational, a priori structures of the mind are fixed, and that it is these formal categories that pre-determine meaning and language.

For Bachelard, the Cartesian-Kantian categories of space and time that structure possible experience are stuck within a "substance-attribute metaphysics" (188) that impedes a genuinely scientific understanding of reality. Relativity theory has already discounted space and time as "insufficiently objective" (Tiles, 189) and quantum mechanics has debunked absolute truth to the less prominent stature of statistical probability. At the micro-physical level, the metaphysics of objectual realism is rejected in favor of a functional dialectic of theory and experiment. The resulting knowledge is not absolute, but "...determined negatively as the limit reached by the elimination of all possible errors" (Tiles, 193). Absolute determination of all physical substances and their attributes is unattainable and objective knowledge is necessarily frustrated and open-ended:

> The whole of the intellectual life of science plays dialectically...at the frontier of the unknown. The very essence of reflection is to understand what one has not understood.[94]

Not only does mathematics refrain from intuitive modes of thought that lay claim to absolute truth; science itself operates with the implicit assumption that the mathematical forms it employs are neither immutable nor expressive of unchanging substances and their attributes. Baconian science, whose concepts linked substantive 'predicates' to pre-existing 'subjects' tantamount to a "...translation manual..." (Tiles, 210) for scientific objectivity - is abandoned by Bachelard. With it is discarded the idea that there exists a "...fixed set of rational categories which must be...realised within space and time..."(Tiles, 211).

Has modern science, then, taken refuge in the radical idealism of metaphysical speculation? According to Bachelard, science's apparent

---
[94] Bachelard, Nouvel Esprit scientifique, pp. 177-178.

return to metaphysics is not a flight from objectual realism. Theoretical concepts, he maintains, while it is true that they cannot "be viewed as applicable to things in themselves..." (Kant, Critique of Pure Reason, (London: Macmillan, 1929(Riga, 1787)), p. 181) must, however, be empirically verifiable by experiment. In order to 'realize' a concept, the scientist must specify the conditions under which it is possible to obtain experimental evidence. And it is neither the subjective concerns of the knower nor the empirical data of observed phenomena that determine these limits. Rather, the "conception...of reality... (and the) "standards of objectivity" (files, 211) that comprise physical theory at a particular point in the evolution of scientific knowledge are what constitute empirical fact. Objective reality is not given - either by direct observation or by deductive reasoning; it is generated out of the systematic process of "metaphysical revision" (Tiles, 213). Science produces a reality that has no 'absolute value'. What can be known objectively is known relative to a frame of reference that determines only

...possible, experimentally mediated experience" (Tiles, 215).

Scientific descriptions, which in the Newtonian worldview recorded phenomena according to discoverable laws of nature, now *produce* phenomena. What is described cannot be "...separated, even conceptually, from the experimental situation which makes the measurement possible and which produces the result" (Tiles, 216). Science must compromise its goal of absolute description of particles and limit itself to a knowledge that is always relative to the experimental procedures and expectations which situate the hypothesis. Bachelard's parting with classical physics and its allegiance to the principles of atomism revolutionizes the status of scientific objectivity. The positing of an ultimate reality whose transcendence solicits the act of knowing is replaced by a new concept of what constitutes reality itself. It is not simply a question of an ultimate "...particle... (being) in a particular state which we can never fully know. (Tiles, 217)" For Bachelard, the objectivity of micro-physics is constituted by the "rational principle" that is the Heisenberg principle (ARPC, 296); the presupposition of an 'absolute' outside the boundaries of applied rationalism is a vestige of outdated metaphysics. Reality is none other than the aggregate of successive approximations of an objectivity that "cannot be finally complete" (Tiles, 218).

Yet if objectivity is defined subjectively as the formal categories that structure the world of experience, it is easy to see how science might fall prey to the criticism that 'reality' is simply that which conforms to the latest theory. By this definition, scientific knowledge reflects the theoretical status quo and lacks the impartiality so readily attributed to science. Bachelard's theory of approximate knowledge neither robs science of its objectivity nor invalidates the veracity of its truth claims. There is not 'scientific knowledge' on the one hand, and knowledge of absolute reality on the other; for, *"ideally* accurate knowledge *is* objective knowledge of reality" (Tiles, 219; italics mine). Science can authenticate its claims to cumulative progress because the notion of progress itself has been redefined as the process of modifying the concept of objectivity.

We have seen how Bachelard has integrated in a novel fashion the previously distinct roles of subject and object, theory and experiment; he has also redrawn the lines of demarcation between form and content in scientific investigation. Just as the inquiring subject alters and is altered in turn by his object, just as the results of experimentation are paradoxically fixed by the parameters of theoretical propositions, so the dynamic of mathematical form and empirical content is called into question. Objectivity is not found in the object of study; it is the product of a dialectical interplay between mathematics and empirical method, both converging on the object as an approximated limit, rather than an absolute given. It is something "...about which there is more, and more accurate, knowledge yet to be gained" (Tiles, 225).

CHAPTER THIRTEEN: EPISTEMOLOGICAL REVOLUTION

The novelty of Bachelard's epistemology of science lies not in its elaboration of the reigning paradigm of relativity, but in the bold assertion that knowledge, though indeterminate and probabilistic, nevertheless possesses an ontological significance. Knowledge of the physical world can never be "absolutely exact" (Smith, 10) despite the precision of formal mathematics, because the scientist's results are always contingent on inexact means of measurement as well as a mathematics that is increasingly abstract. In other words, mathematics' arbitrary relationship with empirical reality and science's methodological and instrumental restrictions preclude absolute certainty about objects. Science no longer presupposes a fixed object of knowledge which will eventually yield to successive attempts at approximation; the absolute certainty that science once presumed to disclose now resides in the process itself rather than in the posited object. This indeterminacy of the object of knowledge has given rise to an 'absolute' of a different breed - the method of approximate knowledge itself. As Bachelard remarks, "truth seems...to refer solely to the procedures of knowledge. It cannot rise above the conditions of its verification" (CA, 231).

The traditional ontology of substance, then, must give way to a "constructed realism" (CA, 187) which has no logical correlation with the empirical world. This constructed knowledge represents no correspondence with objects, but rather its own internal coherence, intuited by the imagination of the scientist himself.[95] The latter is guided by the assumption that "the possible is...the a priori framework of the real" (Bachelard, La Valeur inductive de la relativite, (Paris: Vrin, 1929), p. 81). Bachelard broadens the parameters of relativity, claiming that it "organizes entities (even) before posing...the essentially secondary problem of their reality" (VIR, 213). He exceeds Einstein's own realist interpretation of matter being "...in a sense anterior to space" (VIR, 219) and insists on the role of consciousness and intellect in the structuring of reality. What we know, he maintains, is determined by the formal structures of cognition.

L'Intuition de ('instant (1932) and Les Intuitions atomistiques (1933), while they do belie a nostalgia for metaphysics on the part of the author, remain safely within the confines of philosophy of science. Le Nouvel Esprit scientifique (1934) extends some of the themes of Bachelard's early works on epistemology by insisting on the priority of rational constructs over reality. Scientific realism, Bachelard notes, is an unconventional blend of rationalism and empiricism in which the "epistemological vector seems very clear. It surely goes from the rational to the real and not the reverse - from reality to the

---

[95] Bachelard speaks of the "creative intuition" of the scientist, who mediates the opposing agendas of "logic" and "experiment". Bachelard, Etude sur l'evolution d'un probleme de physique: La propagation thermique dans les solides. Paris, 1928, p. 179.

general" (NES, 4). Modern science's radical realism modifies the criteria for absolute knowledge by shifting the locus of objectivity from a *telos* or final cause to the very process of "transcend(ing) the immediate" (NES, 12). Science yields truth not because it deduces the empirical world from immutable laws of mathematics, but rather in and through its "poetic effort" (NES, 31) to summon a constructed totality out of possible elements.

In <u>Le Nouvel Esprit scientifique,</u> Bachelard endorses Einstein's categorical rejection of absolute space and time. Relativity, together with Heisenberg's uncertainty principle, re-evaluates the conditions of theory (form) and experiment (content), such that the "...experiment itself becomes part of the reality being explored" (Smith, 29). Mathematical physics deals not with absolutes, but with an enigmatic 'intertextuality' of the real and the possible. Reality is "rediscovered as a particular case of the possible" (NES, 58) and science, like poetry, fashions ideas that project a possible construction of reality.

Time, space, form, matter, motion—all the "former absolutes" (Smith, 30) which lent objectivity to classical science—are problematized by modern science's relational paradigm. The scientist no longer thinks reality by submitting data to the universal laws of physics; he imagines the possibility of objects that "...have a reality only in their relations" (NES, 132), themselves relative to the artistic model at hand.[96]

Given Bachelard's elaboration of the "new scientific mind" and its projected[97] reality, and in light of his portrayal of mathematical constructs as "Mallarmean images" (NES, 56), it would seem that he is absolving modern science of any ontological function in the cognitive process whatsoever. Causation, permanence, time and space - all of the "primary qualities"[98] traditionally associated with objective reality, are now understood as mere properties of the formal procedures that structure objectivity (EEPC, 86). In modern physics, the experiment does not "translate...reality: it actualizes a chance" (EEPC, 102); for even the notion of extended, observable space has been replaced with a hypothetical space that is modifiable with each subsequent theory. Bachelard's science of approximation posits a constructed, provisional reality of the here and now, much like Kristevan psychoanalysis proposes possible interpretations that are always phases of a work in progress produced by the therapist and the 'subject in process'.

What then, if any, is the ontological foundation beneath Bachelardian approximate knowledge? If successive approximations draw incrementally

---

[96] Even such prima facie laws as "causality" find themselves reinterpreted in light of relativity. Modern science now reconsiders the relationship of cause and effect to be non-deterministic; it evaluates phenomena as governed by the laws of probability rather than by fixed causality.

[97] Bachelard considers both science and poetry as projections rather than reflections of reality. Smith, p. 30.

[98] As Roch Smith explains, "The constructed phenomena of science, such as electron spin, have no meaning in isolation. One may *imagine* the spin of an isolated electron...but one does not *think* it." Smith, Gaston Bachelard. Boston, G.K. Hall & Company, 1982, p. 30.

closer to but never finally arrive at objective reality, science's dream of a final theory is a chimera. Bachelard justifies the revolutionary realism of the new scientific mind by reproaching classical physics with what he calls the "substantialist seduction" (FES, 111). It is the substantialist myth, so beloved to Western metaphysics, that has captivated science and continues to lure it with promises of the "underlying substance" (Smith, 39) beneath appearances. As long as science continues to buttress its ontological inquiry with metaphysics, it will persist in its naïve faith in a "spatial realism" (Smith, 35). What Bachelard is trying to promote is the novel idea that ontology and change can coexist, that being and nothingness are not mutually exclusive, i.e., that the relative can be 'true'. As Bachelard laments, even language itself is still seduced by the "myth of the interior" (FES, 101). Rules of syntax and the custom of "accumulat(ing) ...adjectives on the same noun" (FES, 111) operate under the assumption of a mysterious, irreducible reality. The modern scientist must relinquish this residual metaphysics and admit that the realism of the method of detection has more objective being than any delusions of an absolute substance (FES, 213).

Despite Bachelard's insistence on the constructive role of scientific knowledge, despite his call for a meta-rationalism that parts company with the absolute reason of classical physics, Bachelard nevertheless preserves the mechanism of transcendence which fueled science's quest for the absolute.

His dialectical "philosophy of no" initiates a new brand of "polemical reasoning" (PN, 119) whose task it is to explain a "super-object" (119) rather than a hidden substance, and which employs rational constructs that "transcend" (Smith, 47) the principles of a priori, deductive reasoning. The realist categories of "object", "rationalism", "ontology" are rewritten as modern science's "super-object", "surrationalism", and "dynamology"[99] all of which seek transcendence in the process of approximating knowledge rather than in the truths of either idealism or realism. Science, Bachelard believes, is no longer the privileged receptacle of ontological truth; yet it continues to be "metaphysically relevant" (Smith, 49) as long as its claims to objectivity are tempered by the formal limits of "surrationalism".

Bachelard's critique of atomism is launched against an obstinate realism that lingers among mainstream philosophers of science as well as critics and scholars outside the scientific enterprise. Until recently, given its status as ultimate substratum of matter, the atom was "...easily taken as the archetype of the independent and immutable object" (Bachelard, Les Intuitions atomistiques (Essai de classification), (Boivin, 1933; Vrin, 2nd ed., 1975), p. 41). Rather than comprehend the atom for what it is - a network of probable relations that are contingent on position and observation - naive realists

---

[99] Also referred to by Bachelard as "restrictive ontology," the term describes the 'probable' ontological status of scientific particles, whose being is determined by method.

assume that the properties observed are reducible to an underlying atomic essence. Yet, Bachelard argues, the atom itself possesses no absolute

attributes intrinsic to it; it is the locus of a "convergence of relations" (IA, 117) that hypothesizes, but does not mandate, the existence of an absolute ontological foundation. The objectivity of the atom, according to Bachelard's account of modern science, resides not in the way it comes to be, but in the way it comes to be known.

In La Dialectique de la duree, Bachelard dispels the unspoken assumption that matter and time are continuous. Continuity, he shows, when applied to both time and space, is merely a convenient metaphor which makes the "anarchy of vibrations... (the) interminable cacophonies" (Bachelard, La Dialectique de la duree, (Boivin, 1936; (P.U.F., Nouvelle edition, 1950), p. 131) of existence tolerable. The only way to escape from the meaningless succession of instants that piece reality is to submit the intellect to what Bachelard calls "cogito 3" - a rigorous, self-reflective act of cognition by which the mind grasps itself 'thinking that it thinks'. This meta-rational activity is divorced from lived human existence and its contingencies, yet for Bachelard it is the closest thing to "the absolute" (Smith, 68).

It is also in the Dialectique de la duree that Bachelard takes the first tentative steps toward a critical reflection on art in its own right. Unlike psychoanalysis, which with few exceptions (e.g., Kristeva) views art solely as a last resort for the sexual drive" (DD, 141). Poetry like that of Valery intrigues him with its ability to freeze the flow of time in an "immobilized moment"[100] where a fleeting glimpse of the "absolute" (Smith, 68) is conjured through images of vertical time.[101] Yet even as he is haunted by the charms of "Baudelairian correspondences" (DD, xi) of reason and art, Bachelard remains the staunch rationalist whose admiration of poetry only serves to reinforce his conviction that thought has entered a new era. Surrationalism, much like surrealism, has "...left the shores of immediate reality..." (Smith, 69), allowing reason and poetry to "converge" (69) in a collaborative effort to restructure experience. When Bachelard muses that poetry might be "the very principle of creative evolution... (and that) man might have a poetic destiny... "(DD, xi), he is begrudgingly admitting the possibility that art, as an aesthetic activity apart from science, may have an ontological *raison d'être*. At this early stage, however, Bachelard is unwilling to commit himself to a full-blown metaphysics of the imagination and leaves the door to "being" only half-open, continuing to focus on reason as the architect of knowledge.

---

[100] Bachelard, "The Poetic Moment and the Metaphysical Moment," The Right to Dream. New York, 1971, p. 202.
[101] Paul Valery's "Graveyard by the Sea," exemplifies the poet's identification of images of verticality with the absolute: "Temple of Time, I a single sigh resumed/To this pure pitch ascending/ I attune Myself, surrounded by a gazing sea..." Valery, "Le Cimetiere Marin," ed. Graham D. Martin, Austin: University of Texas Press, 1971, p. 43.

CHAPTER FOURTEEN: DIALECTICAL ABSOLUTE

Bachelard coined the term "discursive idealism" or "open Kantianism" to describe the status of knowledge as neither exclusively determined by a rational subject, nor completely conditioned by "something other than itself" (Jones, 7). This "not-self" (Bachelard, <u>Etude sur l'evolution d'un probleme de physique,</u> p. 92) is unlike both the thing-in-itself of German idealism and the brute reality of British empiricism. Out of the complicity of reason and reality, self and other, knowledge is born: the knower investigates something "other than" himself and that "other" in turn changes him. Bachelard joins hands with modem science in desacralizing the Cartesian subject; "...no longer sovereign, no longer autonomous...and unchanging, [the subject is]... transcended...recreated by" (Jones, 7) the not-self.

The reciprocity of reason and reality which poetry has heralded and modem science has adopted as its heuristic model demands a total relinquishing of the preconceptions of both rationalism and materialism. Reason is no longer the supreme arbiter of truth, yet empirical inquiry is no more capable than reason of revealing the absolute. Bachelard maintains a calculated balance between upholding reason as an ordering principle in cognition, and recognizing that reason has no epistemological monopoly on truth. He prevents the dissolution of the thinking subject, all the while refusing to accept the facile solutions of idealism.

In the chapter "On Knowledge and Description" of his <u>Essai sur la</u>

connaissance approchee, Bachelard tackles the problem of how to "...reject idealism without also rejecting the subject... "(Jones, 15). The act of cognition is comprised of two poles - the knower and the known - and knowledge is like an "alternating current oscillating between" (CA, 260) them. The scientist cannot afford to be smug or self-satisfied in his knowledge of reality, because reality itself is constantly engaging him in "endless polemics" (Jones, 16). Truth is not waiting to be discovered through the lenses of reason's a priori deductive system. Mind and reality are co-dependent and the subject is simultaneously frustrated and tempted by the obstinacy of the "not-self - the transcendent other" (Jones, 16).

What is the precise nature of this mutuality between mind and reality? According to Bachelard it is one of neither correspondence nor mimesis, but of difference. Reason will not ultimately conform to a "given, fixed reality" (Michel Vadee, Bachelard ou le nouvel idealisme epistemologique, (Paris: Editions Sociales, 1975), pp. 46-50), yet neither is it exiled from a "neverto-be-attained goal" (Smith, 12). The scientific mind confronts error in the form of failure, lack of precision, and incompleteness; it is precisely this meeting of reason and difference that supplies the impetus for knowledge (CA, 249). Error is that which allows the knower to accept the truth, however humbling, that reality is reluctant to reveal itself, that it is ultimately inexhaustible. It is the "undeniable existence of error," claims Bachelard, "...which obliges us to make do with approximations" (275). Mind and reality may occasionally intersect in glimpses of scientific progress, but always in and through the "twists and turns of approximation" (Jones, 20).

It is ironic that an intransigent, inaccessible reality is the very source of transcendence that inspires reason to pursue its mysteries. Reason in contemporary science becomes problematized, reflecting the "subtlety, richness, and diversity" (CA, 92) of an object that remains irrational. The allure and fascination of a recalcitrant reality operate on the mind such that it is transformed by the "diversity and multiplicity of phenomena" (43). For Bachelard, then, the modern absolute is to be sought neither in the myth of a knowable reality nor in the sovereignty of reason, but in the "fundamental incompleteness of knowledge..." (Bachelard in Jones, 24).

L'Intuition de l'instant, with its theme of time and consciousness, seems like an abrupt departure from an uninterrupted series of texts on the philosophy of science. Yet a more subtle analysis of the work places it squarely in the mainstream of Bachelardian thought.[102] In it Bachelard confesses his conversion to "an awareness of the poetic dimension of existence" (1969, 56),

---

[102] It is Jones who argues that "L'Intuition de l'instant" is merely a "reaffirmation" of Bachelard's mission to apply to the fullest possible extent the result of scientific developments.

although this "desire for poetry" (81) has already appeared in embryonic form in a previous book, La Valeur inductive de la relativite (1929). It is in this latter work that Bachelard first expounds on the radical nature of the "epistemological break" (Jones, 28) which Einstein's theory of relativity precipitated. Relativity's restructuring of the relation between mind and reality necessitates an unequivocal rupture with "habits of thought where absolutes are concerned" (Jones, 28). The absolutes of both realism and idealism have been demystified by relativity, which denies that either subject or object be treated independently from the relations through which they are observed.

In Essai sur la connaissance approchee, Bachelard's thinking maintains a disarming tension between a rejection of absolute duration and a confirmation of the absolute of the instance of consciousness. According to Bachelard, subject and object are engaged in a polemical dynamic in which both are relativized by the onslaught of multiple instants of consciousness. Yet, while relativity has "destroyed the absoluteness of that which has duration..."(Bachelard in Jones, 33), the instant of consciousness displays, nevertheless, the "character of something fixed and absolute" (Jones, 34). Time as an abstraction is a figment of the intellect; in actuality the mind itself weaves the fabric of duration" (Jones, 37) through the creative ordering of instants. The mind cannot encounter absolute uniformity, since it is the mind itself that places instants in sequence along a "path of richness, not of simplicity" (38). The proliferation of new instants that refuse to congeal into a reassuring permanence is an enticing call to the intellect to "reach the limits of experience" (38). Here, at the limits of thought, reason becomes acutely aware of its own delinquency; paradoxically, it is the "irrational" (Jones, 38)-not a salvific absolute- which wakens the knower from his cognitive slumber, beckoning him to confront a new problematical relationship between thought and reality. Bachelard's absolute emerges as a "curious and idiosyncratic amalgam of mathematics and metaphysics" (Jones, 38) - a fractious dyad of reason and being.

Bachelard's metaphysical considerations become increasingly tolerant of a transcendent reality. His attempt to break out of the subject-object antinomy provokes the search for a new category which would explain the dialectic of reason and reality that modern science enforces. Such a concept – "project" - avoids both the metaphysical presuppositions of the subject-object dualism and the realist assumptions of an empirical 'given'. The Bachelardian project is "above the subject and beyond the immediate object" (Bachelard in Jones, 42). By determining that contemporary science is founded on a project, Bachelard bridges the "gulf" (43) that historically has estranged the knower from the object of knowledge. At the same time he suggests that absolute knowledge lies not in the unreachable "thing-in-itself" (e.g., the indivisible sub-atomic particle), but in the dialectical relationship between the scientific mind and the transcendent reality into which he is thrown or 'projected'.

Bachelard is impartial in his criticism of rationalism and realism as epistemological models. There is no immediate intuition "that would establish at a stroke the foundations of reality" nor are there "absolute and definitive" (in Jones, 52) rational categories from which ultimate knowledge can be deduced. The scientist "takes up his position at the crossroads...between realism and rationalism" (Jones, 52) - between an inexhaustible reality that incites his thought and the conceptual apparatus that reason invents. Neither one illuminates eternal truth yet each projects a path toward transcendence. The new objectivity of modern science is never "something immediate and given... (but rather) a difficult pedagogical task... "(in Jones, 53). And, just as subject and object are reborn as a "project" that transcends each of them, so the relationship between phenomena and noumena are re-termed "phenomeno-technique" by Bachelard. The 'either/or' polarity of phenomena and noumena, he claims, cannot logically contain the "alternating movement" of reason and reality progressing toward the "realization of the noumenon"(54).

If objectivity is not a certain goal but a grueling "pedagogical task" that appears to dilute absolute knowledge to 'approximation' and 'successive rectification,' it would seem that Bachelard does not even consider the possibility of satisfied knowledge. Yet in one of his most compelling works, Les Intuitions atomistiques, he refers to the cathartic effects of the new scientific mind; in removing itself from the safe harbor of immediate reality, the intellect heals itself of the "psychological hardening" (Jones, 87) that common sense has induced. He even speaks of modern science as a therapeutic "psychoanalysis of Euclidian impulses" (42) that purges the mind of the diseased habits of "good sense" (14). The epistemological angst of a quest that is always tortured by incompleteness finds consolation in the "mental hygiene"(88) of a healthy mind.

It is in the 1936 text, La Dialectiaue de la duree, that Bachelard introduces the quasi-mystical concept of "cogito cubed" - i.e., a plane of consciousness that is beyond both common sense and the scientific project. To "live temporally at the power of three...—(to) think that I think that I think" (Jones, 61)-- exceeds the rigour of polemical thought (cogito squared) and enters the realm of pure consciousness. Within this induced state of radical interiority, the mind is not consciousness of objects or of a transcendent 'other', but only of itself as "pure project...transcended by difference latent within....by the other that is our self" (Jones, 62).[103] Bachelard ventures even further into the confines of metaphysics, declaring that consciousness at the power of three is experienced outside the psyche, in the temporal zone of 'vertical time'. Only at this level of consciousness and in this experience of time is the thinking subject truly

---

[103] Similar to the Kristevan notion of "strangers to ourselves". Kristeva, Etrangers a nous-memes. Paris, 1988.

authentic, as a "self that is ever renewed, ever different" (Jones, 63). Curiously, he finds, it is the upheaval and turmoil of vertical time that brings the stillness of repose.

Bachelard's cogito cubed is the closest he dares to speculate on the possibility of an absolute - his perplexing hybrid of science and contemplation (Jones, 64-65), metaphysics and psychoanalysis, identity and difference. Here, while "thinking ourselves as someone who is thinking" (in Jones, 68), "spiritualized" (68) being enters into the "first really unballasted state in which consciousness of formal life brings us a special kind of happiness" (in Jones, 69). Bachelard's contemplative state of intellectual repose begs the question of the constitution of his absolute: rational or spiritual, intellectual or intuitive? He does not hesitate to conclude that the absolute of vertical time straddles both categories, as a "purely aesthetic kind of thought... (in which) mental and spiritual life will become pure aesthetics" (Bachelard in Jones, 70).

CHAPTER FIFTEEN: REASON AND REVERIE

Bachelard's philosophy of science develops themes which parallel some of the fundamental tenets of his theory of the imagination. Common to both is the valorization of the dynamic, "shifting" [104] character of the intellect, as well as the rejection of a priori truths in favor of "the essential mobility"[105] of thought when it is free of "epistemological obstacles" (Colette Gaudin, "L'Imagination et le reverie: Remarques sur la poetique de Gaston Bachelard," Symposium 20, (1966), p. xi). Yet, in the same breath Bachelard is unequivocal in his surveying of the boundaries that separate science and poetry; each one, he claims, corresponds to a distinct dimension and orientation of the human psyche. Man's "double nature" (in Gaudin, xii) is comprised of *animus* (reason) and *anima* (imagination); the two poles alternate in a rhythmic pattern that precludes static truth and mobilizes thought. He is adamant that the "...axes of poetry and science are opposed from the start" (Bachelard, The Psychoanalysis of Fire, 9-15) and that poetry's lyrical "effusion" (9-15) must be restrained from the "taciturnity" (9-15) of the scientific mind. Notwithstanding Bachelard's insistence that "between concept and image there is no possibility of synthesis" (PR, 45-47), he concedes that it is a "hunger for images" (Gaudin, xiv) that fuels the impulse for seeking knowledge. Ultimately—although critics are divided on the issue of

---
[104] Jones defines this shifting as "an ability to shake off intellectual habits....(xi)" Bachelard borrows the term from Alfred Korzybski in "Science and Sanity: An Introduction to Non-Aristotelian Systems and General Semantics," (New York: The International Non-Aristotelian Library Compnay, 1933).

[105] Not a "superficial mobility which replaces one concept with another" arbitrarily, but an "internal dialectic" which dissolves fixed concepts and refreshes the "ambivalence and freedom" of language." (Jones, xi-xii).

whether Bachelard underwent a "conversion" (Gaudin, xv) to reverie—it is imagination and not reason, he concludes, that engages the highest potential of the mind (PF, 215).

Bachelard's poetics promotes a Proustian belief in the fundamental correspondence between mind and reality that is illuminated by the material imagination. He goes beyond Proustian metaphysics, however, in attributing an "archetypal energy" (Gaudin, xix) to the material elements and assigning them to a psychology of the imagination. Bachelard dissolves the subject-object dichotomy of metaphysics by redefining matter as the "mother-substance" (PS, xxxiv), which orients the psyche to the real world. The four fundamental elements of the material universe-earth, air, fire, and water-incite the intellect to enter into a sympathetic union with that which is most essential in the object. Bachelard's material imagination marks a bold departure from western metaphysics, with its privileging of 'forms' or 'ideas' over matter. Materiality is not an inferior substratum that 'participates' in an ideal form; it is rather the "mirror of our energy" (Bachelard, La Terre et les reveries de la volonte: Essai sur ('imagination des forces, (Corti, 1948), p. 23). Bachelard inverts the hierarchy of metaphysics by attributing to materiality the essential quality of depth, and to formal images the status of superficiality. It is by "think(ing) matter" (AS, 14) that the imagination ushers in the real, by virtue of making it less 'real' in the habitual sense of the term. He has in fact introduced a metaphysics of matter - in flagrant defiance of philosophy's arguable privileging of the absolute as *Idea*. Immediate experience is grasped most completely neither by rigorous observation nor by the application of formal concepts, but by engaging the mind to the "function of unreality" (Gaudin, xxvii). Bachelard believes that to be deprived of the unreal - the imaginary - is a form of neurosis which prevents the flourishing of the "happy being" (in Gaudin, xxvii).

The faculty of the imagination is traditionally associated with the free play of images and things, unencumbered by the prerequisites of realism. For Bachelard, imagination is elevated to an ontological role in integrating the most profound features of reality, becoming a "synthesizing force for human existence" (PR 107). The elements of the material imagination are not arbitrarily paired with reality; on the contrary, they "...dream in agreement with the becoming of an element" (Gaudin, xxviii). The human psyche is equipped with archetypal categories that lend validity and permanence to the material imagination by connecting the mind to the being of objects. By extracting the essential qualifies of objects—beyond their observed or reasoned characteristics—imagination awakens the collective unconscious of nature. It is in and through this profoundly material gesture that the "world opens and rises in the movement of images" (Gaudin, xxx). For Bachelard, there is transcendence in depth, permanence in movement, absolute reality in the apparently unreal.

Bachelard's "material imagination," like the Romantic and Surrealist movements, exalts the poetic[106] dimension of the mind and its affinity for a symbolic reality of correspondences. If "matter is the unconscious of form" (Bachelard, L'Eau et les reves, p. 70), he reasons, it would follow that substances themselves are possessed of "affective values" (Gaudin, xxx) which the poetic mind can solicit through the language of reverie. Yet despite his belief in an underlying complicity between mind and reality, Bachelard is careful to clarify that the unconscious dimension of reality dwells within the substance as the product of a contentious relationship between opposing qualities within matter. The affective quality within a substance (e.g., 'air' or verticality), rather like an inchoate force or proto-substance, confronts its opposite quality and it is this productive tension that inspires the poetics of matter. Poetic language voices the contradictions underlying the presumably

---

[106] I use the term "poetic" in the sense of "*poiesis*" - referring to the imagination's dynamic, self-generative process.

real world of perception and makes it aesthetically plausible to entertain incompatible images such as "the blackness of milk" (Gaudin, xxxii).[107]

Bachelard's theory of animated objects which unite with the "...deepest organic aspects of consciousness" (TR, 81) challenges the traditional concept of metaphysical correspondence, according to which all contingencies are absorbed by an essence or absolute. For Bachelard, images are "...incapable of repose" (PS, 36); they never conform to a singular theme, but flaunt a "...daring, proliferating sensuousness, intoxicated with inexactitude" (TR, 81). He dismisses psychoanalysis' theory of the maternal archetype as too reductive; for, it would be "too simple if the greatest of all archetypes...obliterated the life of all the others" (FR, 122). The raw affectivity that poetry unlocks within substances becomes, paradoxically, a new order emerging from chaos. The contradicting forces that preclude a unified poetic image are the very forces that "plumb the depths of being....(to) seek at once the primitive and eternal" (ER,). It is, then, in the irony of a 'dynamic unity' that Bachelard finds his absolute, not in the clean lines of the formal imagination.'[108] In his estimation, aesthetics has become impoverished by an excessive reliance on visible forms; only material imagination can pierce the formal shell

---

[107] It is not absurd to speak of the blackness of milk, if one feels that white "becomes" white by repulsing blackness....(Gaudin, p. xxxii). It is by virtue of the fact that "whiteness" is at the same time "not black" that reality is dialectical, and it is this tension within a substance that fascinates.

[108] Bachelard distinguishes between formal and material imagination in L'Eau et les reves. The former confines itself to the "fixed images which offer themselves to perception." (Gaudin, p. xxxvi) and produces "...only superficial beauty..." while the latter unearths "the very root of the image-producing force." (TR, pp. 1-4)

of substances, and retrieve "...behind the visible images the hidden one... "(ER, 1-4). Unlike idealist philosophies, with their emphasis on the sublimating function of the rational mind, Bachelard's material imagination reasserts the primacy of the "vegetative and material forces" (ER, 1-4). Matter is not simply an indeterminate 'base' which must be rationalized by an absolute 'superstructure' in order to acquire meaning; matter is meaningful in its own right, "...imbued with values in two directions: in the direction of depth, and in the direction of height" (ER, 1-4). In both orientations, Bachelard admits the reality of an indefinable absolute: in depth, as "something unfathomable, as a mystery" (1-4); and in height, as an "inexhaustible force, as a miracle" (1-4).

Bachelard's faith in the power of the reflective mind to "...thrust...far beyond the line of life" (<u>La Dialectique de la duree,</u> (1950), pp. 96-103, in Gaudin, p. 70)" confirms his commitment to the idea that human existence is intimately bound to the absolute. Yet the 'unfathomable mystery' which he alludes to above conforms to none of our metaphysical or theological preconceptions of the absolute. Neither completely material or spiritual, rational or intuitive, discursive or lyrical but a curious admixture of all, the Bachelardian absolute seems amorphous at best. Likewise, the epistemological method that is most suited to this absolute is neither exclusively cognitive, nor entirely literary. Only a "purely *aesthetic* kind of *thought* (italics mine)" (La Dialectique de la duree, 96-103) - the coupling of science and art - allows the mind to live "at the level of cogito cubed" (96-103); i.e., to surpass the intellectual and imaginative barriers of ordinary life. And finally, it is not the methodic composure of rational thought that creates happiness; it is the "active repose... (of the) lyric state... "(DD, 148-50) that binds heart and mind in "pleasure" and "solace"(148-50).

How can a state of poetic repose transcend the indeterminacy of human existence? Bachelard carefully distinguishes unbridled poetic ecstasy from the "mental elaboration" (DD, 148-50) of the lyrical state which he recommends. When art is structured and informed by reason, then the mind reaches a "truly intellectual lyric state" (148-150). Furthermore, it is not enough for the mind to intuit the sensuality of the poem; one must "think...poetry" so as to "reveal all its charms" (148-50). Reading poetry, for Bachelard, is as illuminating as a micro-physical experiment; both extricate thought from its staid conventions and participate in "constructing difference" (Gaudin, 76). In both, the flat contours of immediate reality are cloaked in the "...rich garment of conditionals" (DD, 148-50). Rational knowledge is enhanced by the adventure of the mind as it flirts with possibility (Gaudin, 74).

CHAPTER SIXTEEN: FROM SCIENCE TO POETRY

1938 marks a transitional year for Bachelard, with the publication of La Formation de l'esprit scientifique and La Psychanalyse du feu. While mainstream critics maintain that his conversion to poetry is never wholehearted (Gaudin, Gaston Bachelard ou la conversion de l'imaginaire, (Paris: Marcel Riviere, 1969), pp. 79-81), it is virtually uncontested that after 1938 Bachelard favors the poetic orientation. His newfound interpretation of consciousness as " Thoroughly prejudiced... [by] preconceived ideas and values" (Gaudin, 79) prompts him to explore the implications of an intuitive, affective dimension of the mind that may condition, if not determine, thought. Bachelard seems more prepared to accept the predominance of an unconscious - an "instinctual, affective part of us" (Gaudin, 80) - which is more often than not the stimulus for knowledge. The intuitive, irrational part of the psyche is thus a credible cognitive mode in its own right. And its resultant knowledge, however truthful or correct, is "...like a light which always casts a shadow in some nook or cranny ...never immediate, never complete" (FES, 1314). Bachelard does not recant his original assertion that "thought rules our being...[that] consciousness...constitutes our truth" (L' Intuition de ('instant, 71); yet this same rational activity is now girded with an emotional, psychological basis. The scientist implements "experiment and technique" in order to realize "some modification *already brought into being psychologically* (italics mine)"(FES, 244-49). It is this valorization of psychological intuition that compels Bachelard the philosopher of science to exploit the less rigorous but equally inspiring dimension of the literary imagination.

While already having insisted, as we have seen, on the "clear polarity of intellect and imagination" (PR, 45), Bachelard at this juncture seems willing to temper the rigid dualism of science and poetry. Poetry, he writes in Instant poetique et instant metaphysique (1939), should "give us both a view of the world and the secret of a soul" (Bachelard, The Right to Dream, (New York: Grossman, 1971), p. 224); it is at once an emanation of subjectivity and an objective rendering of reality. The "shifting and breaching of (the) familiar frontiers" (Gaudin, 92) that have always kept subject and object respectfully at odds makes room for an acknowledgement of science and poetry as two opposing yet mutually enriching activities.

At a time when Bachelard had established his reputation and tenure as a noted epistemologist and philosopher of science at the Sorbonne, he launches into four groundbreaking books on poetry, L'Eau et les reves (1942), L'Air et les songes (1943), La Terre et les reveries de la volonte (1948), and La Terre et les reveries du repos (1948). Gilbert Durand has sung his praises as the critic who "obliged French thinkers for the first time to take imagination seriously" (Durand, Les Structures anthropologiques de l'imaginaire, (Paris: Bordas, 1969), pp. 15-27, 31-32, 45-46). La Psychanalyse du feu is generally considered to be the turning point in Bachelard's career; for it is in this text, which Bachelard dismisses as "both disorderly and incomplete" (in C.G. Christofides, "Bachelard's Aesthetics," Journal of Aesthetics and Art Criticism, No. 20, (1962), p. 267), that he retracts his initial statement that science is the sole purveyor of truth. He now makes room for a "poetic truth" (Gaudin, 94) that later in his thought proves to be more comprehensive, yet more perplexing than scientific truth. It is a truth that has the authority of law (Bachelard later renames it the "law of the four elements" (ER, 4)) that was previously reserved for reason, yet challenges the very autonomy that reason guarantees. The four elemental archetypes that determine poetic images and human reverie in general - earth, air, fire, and water - exert a fascination over the mind such that the poet and reader of poetry are drawn to them by "an unconscious affinity". [109]It is this affective link to matter which seems to challenge the liberty of the rational mind proclaimed by science; as we shall see, the threat of biological and material determinacy is not a serious one for Bachelard, who finds in the law of the four elements the path to the highest human freedom.

---

[109]Mary McAllester Jones, Gaston Bachelard, Subversive Humanist, Madison: University of Wisconsin Press, 1991, p. 94.

n suggesting that the literary imagination is governed by fundamental material archetypes, Bachelardian poetics recalls Freudian psychoanalysis and its theory of the drives. Both Freud and Bachelard establish the priority of the unconscious, imaginary dimension of existence; yet for Bachelard, Freud's conclusion that behavior is determined by the libidinal impulses of the unconscious is a gross simplification of the complex relationship between mind and matter. Against Freud's sexual reductionism, Bachelard situates the source of poetic truth in the "intermediate zone" (PF, 26, 32) midway between the unconscious and the rational, prior to objective knowledge. The poetic mind's relationship with matter is "intellectually charged" (Gaudin, 94) and material imagination does not flourish in a stupor of reverie[110] but propels itself by a "will to intellectuality" (PF, 26).

As he does in his epistemological works, Bachelard urges the reader to think beyond the traditional categories that have paraded themselves as absolutes by perception and custom. Both science and poetry, he insists, call for a "rupture and a conversion" (Bachelard, Lautreamont, (Paris: Jose Corti, 1939), p. 155), transcending immediate experience in favor of creating what he calls "superobjects" (La Philosophie du non, (1940), p. 139). The material images that together form an oneiric base of poetic truth incite the poetic

---

110 For Bachelard, "reverie" is synonymous with "poetic imagination". Reverie does not correspond to daydreaming, but the "free play of the mind around objects," (Gaudin, p. 95). The subject is always present in reverie, in a "glimmer of consciousness."

mind to "...go beyond the human condition" (NES, 23) by indulging in new forms of imaginary thought. Underlying the superficial forms that imagination has stockpiled is an imagined matter" (TR, 173-177) which draws the mind to a "substance of the depths"(TR, 173-177). The absolute—"...the world beyond the phenomenon..."(TR, 173-177)—is buried by traditional images of sensation, but revealed in all its elusive mystery[111] through the material imagination. Imagination is the "new literary mind" (ER, 173-177) which, like the new scientific mind, is unencumbered by the idealist-realist dichotomy, for it is at once subjective and objective. "Never content with just one plane of reality" (173-177), the literary image surveys the broad spectrum of human experience, from the "organic to the mental and spiritual... "(ER, 173-177).

Bachelard's studies on contemporary philosophy of science have established "applied rationalism" and the theory of approximate knowledge as bastions of the new scientific mind. As we have shown, for Bachelard reason is neither an absolute concept from which final principles of knowledge are deduced, nor is it an inductive tool for accumulating empirical data in a totalizing theory of truth. Modern science's modus operandi implodes traditional rational categories by submitting scientific inquiry to a hyper-rationalism or "surrationalism" - an epistemological paradigm that abolishes the clear-cut frontiers between subject and object, mind and reality. Absolute

---
[111] Bachelard claims in this same work that there can be no reverie without ambivalence (Gaudin, p. 102).

knowledge is no longer the goal of scientific inquiry and objectivity is the epiphenomenal product of thought and word. Cogito cubed, with its reflective, critical detachment from immediate reality, restores the mind's sense of well-being and provides "excellent mental hygiene" (NES, 88) for a rational faculty that is easily corrupted by delusions of absolute knowledge.

However "healthy" (Gaudin, 111) modern science may make the mind, Bachelard, in the latter part of his life and work, seeks refuge in poetry as a more authentic way of going "beyond the human condition" (ER, 23). While science may allow us to expand the inventory of knowledge, dispensing with immediate perception and common sense, poetry touts the imagination as a superhuman faculty (ER, 23). Though "surrationalism" may take the mind beyond the limits of Cartesian reason, poetry takes the self beyond even its own humanity. Poetry's images "shatter ready-made phrases" (Bachelard, L'Air et les songes, p. 285) and expose the polysemic core of language - its "sonority, its polyphony" (Gaudin, 115). As we shall see, this explosive, revolutionary dimension of literary language is what frees the mind from the conventions of "received meanings" (Gaudin, 115) and ultimately leads to a transubstantiation of the mind.[112]

The psycho-spiritual transformation which poetry effects signifies a

---

[112] Bachelard states that "the chief function of poetry is to transform us." (L'Eau et les reves) Poetic language no longer represents immutable truths; rather it shifts words and images, creating ambivalent meanings which defy an absolute grasping of truth.

departure from the idealist tradition introduced by Plato. The mind does not gain access to a higher reality by virtue of its participation in eternal forms; nor is it through the contemplation of reason that the absolute Ideas are grasped. For Bachelard, there is always and already an archetypal communion with the privileged liminal images that correspond to the "materializing reverie" (ER, 29-35) of the poetic mind. Thus it is in an essentially material way that the imagination is able to penetrate an otherwise opaque reality, unearthing the hidden "relatedness" (Gaudin, 118) within matter. The elementary poetics Bachelard has catalogued - air, water, earth, and fire - are endowed a priori with an imaginary "density" (ER, 29-35) that distinguishes them from the poetic forms "that belong only to surfaces" (29-35). If the literary mind can "dream deeply" (29-35), imagine beyond formal images to the less ephemeral, material images that a true "poetic force" (29-35) unleashes, then it will have reached the "oneiric sincerity" (L'Air et les songes, 49-53) that for Bachelard ensures the highest psychic fulfillment.

Bachelard's critical reading of Shelley's Prometheus Unbound determines the material image of air to be the most 'oneirically sincere' in explicating the meaning of the text. Shelley's work is replete with aerial images that invoke a "force of psychic elevation" (AS, 49-53) and at the same time expose the "innermost depths" (49-53) of human life. Vertical images of "dizzying arches suspended in the air" and "mountainous ruins" are symbolic of the spiraling "vertigo" (AS, 49-53) of human aspiration as it "strains toward the heights... "(49-53) in hopes of liberation. Bachelard agrees with Shelley that the poet's mission is to resurrect those cosmic images that reconcile man with the "fundamental forces" (L'Air et les songes, 49-53) of the psyche. The essential activity of the mind is not to represent the objective world, but to "...seek the heights... (and) to live...at the summit of being" (49-53). Paradoxically, it is through an imaginary, archetypal affinity with a cosmic element of nature (i.e., air) that the mind becomes super-natural, that it thinks beyond empirical reality to the ethereal realm of the meta-physical. Bachelard informs us that the primary images that the poetic mind rescues from the jaded "images of perception" (TR, 149-54) are meant to awaken the mind out of its realist slumber. Comfortable in our assumption that language corresponds to objects and that its meaning is fixed by history and custom, we are called by poetry to revel in the ambivalence of even the language of technical jargon. The "realist value" (149-54) of words is not their denotative meaning -- their immediate, practical usage—but the oneiric depth that harbors the latent "possibilities of matter" (Gaudin, 133). [113]

---

113 Trade words used to describe the tempering process of the smithy at the same time suggest the internal, moral battle of the hero who unleashes the "trapped fire" within iron. (Gaudin, pp. 149-154).

CHAPTER SEVENTEEN

INTERTEXTUALITY: RETURN TO RATIONALISM

Bachelard's literary sabbatical is abruptly interrupted for an unanticipated return to epistemology. Critics have speculated [114] that perhaps his friendship with the war hero, Jean Cavailles, reanimated in him the faith in science as a "human creation" (ER, 189)[115] and not simply a technical enterprise. In his conference paper entitled "La Vocation scientifique et l'Ame humaine," delivered in Geneva in 1952, Bachelard buttresses his commitment to science, praising its "human value" (29). Modern man, he claims, cannot choose to do without science, for he is "situated in" (pp. 11, 17) it. The danger of abusing scientific knowledge to accommodate political structures is a very real one, but Bachelard remains convinced that if scientific progress is valued primarily for its cognitive worth, it can fulfill the vocation (Gaudin, 136) of human nature.

---

114 Gaudin suggests that Cavailles' work on the philosophy of modern mathematics, Sur la Logique et la theorie de la science (1947), inspired Bachelard to reconsider the "importance of science not as something useful...but as an activity of the mind." (Gaudin, p. 136)

115 Bachelard wrote the preface to Gabriele Ferriere's essay "Jean Cavailles, philosophe et combattant (1903-1944)." (Paris: P.U.F., 1972, pp. 178-190.)

Le Nouvel Esprit scientifique, Essai sur la connaissance approchee, and La Philosophie du non had already opened the gulf between traditional philosophy with its concept of a priori reason, and the "applied" rationalism - auto-productive and open-ended — of contemporary science. Despite their pioneering theories, these earlier works continue to invoke the Enlightenment premise of "the rationalism of identity" (MR, 224): the notion that an individual "ego" thinks contiguously with other independent rational minds. In more recent works, Bachelard introduces the notions of "cogitamus", "divided subject" and "co-rationalism" (Gaudin, 139) - all expressive of his re-evaluation of the scientific enterprise as a dynamic, polemical structure, rather than a solitary venture. Absolute knowledge is no longer the product of the "cogito", a "lone figure, working in his laboratory without companions"(RA, 137); there is a dialectical relationship not only between reason and reality (science), or imagination and matter (poetry), but between "rational regions" (RA, 122) that modify each other. Because an individual mind poses a question against an epistemological context that conditions him and readies him for knowledge, we can no longer speak of aggregate minds but of "the union of intellects" (in Gaudin, 139). We can no longer look to a rational and/or divine essence that precedes existence; rather, we must accomodate the notion of "thinking coexistence (that) precedes existence" (in Gaudin, 139). Once again we must entertain the possibility that Bachelard is entertaining the idea of an a priori absolute, albeit one that is compatible with the social epistemology of applied rationalism. Is he simply replacing the Absolute—Reason, Being or God--with the more modernist but equally idealist concept of "cogitamus"? Bachelard anticipates such criticism, in reminding us that the scientific reality in which we are situated is not "absurd or gratuitous" (Gaudin, 139) but one that we continually formulate by choice; it is a "social reality" (RA, 6) that exists "for-us" (MR, 198) and empowers us. Just as the early Bachelard credited modern science with resolving the subject-object dilemma through the highest exercise of the intellect ("surrationalism"), here Bachelard admits that by individual participation in the "union of minds in the truth" (in Gaudin, 142), science absolves itself of intellectual hubris — of the "desire to be...absolute" (Gaudin, 142). The rational mind transcends immediate reality by thinking beyond the I-Thou dichotomy of rationalist thought; by tethering self and other as two poles within consciousness, the subject is "raised to superexistence... (to) coexistence through apodicticity" (RA, 56-60).[116]

Bachelard is ever mindful of the role of intellectual humility in seeking

---

116 Bachelard emphasizes the role of teaching in cognition. "Surprise, so useful in scientific culture, cannot remain individual. We learn in order to surprise others (RA pp. 56-60)." It is this desire to teach by surprising others out of their "dogmatic slumbers" that will constantly renew the intellect.

knowledge. The mind's will-to-power must be tempered by a vigilant sensitivity to the intertextuality of subject and object; it is never simply "I" who knows, it is "I" and "other" engaged in an epistemological dialogue out of which both emerge changed beings. Science alone, claims Bachelard, can "...establish the mind's dialectical powers, and make the divided subject conscious of its division..."(RA, 66-68). By allowing the mind to hold itself under critical scrutiny- to "understand that we understand" (66-68)--consciousness engages in multiple levels of self-reflection and "surveillance" (77-81) and, as such, can admit that subject and object, mind and reality, are mutually defining.

Bachelard is particularly generous in his praise of "surveillance cubed", a meta-critical activity of the mind by which the method of knowledge itself is surveyed. A more abstract critique, surveillance cubed disputes the absolute character of method and reduces a particular formal model to "...a moment in the progress of method in general" (Bachelard, Rationalisme applique, pp. 77-81)." Bachelard likens the most speculative form of exponential surveillance -surveillance to the fourth power- to a "spiritual exercise" (77-81): its mental discipline, if exercised appropriately, would exceed the parameters of rationalism itself and would aspire to "transcend" (77-81) normative models of mind. A hyper-rational function of the most supreme intellect, cogito-4 is better left, Bachelard warns us, to poetry or "in a very special kind of philosophical meditation" (77-81). It is here, in a zone of extra-temporal lucidity, that the mind may encounter "a fifth element, a luminous, ethereal element... "(77-81). And it is in this extreme state of mental acuity and detachment from reality that the self is truly liberated:

> At moments like this, we really have the impression that there is no longer anything that rises from the depths, nor anything Impulsive (sic), or determined by some destiny that springs from our origins.[117]

Bachelard's reference to "depths", "origins" and impulses can only represent the material, unconscious substratum that threatens the subject with physical determinism. Once freed from an overbearing body, the self can cultivate an appreciation of the "extraordinary human value" (Bachelard, L'Engagement rationaliste, p. 58) of science. A truly modern science is one that fulfills the critical requirements of the first three exponents of surveillance; it is sustained by the two-fold belief that the scientist "...makes science" (Gaudin, 154) at the same time that he is shaped by science.

---

[117] Bachelard, Rationalisme applique, pp. 77-81.

CHAPTER EIGHTEEN: TEMPERED RATIONALISM

Bachelard concludes his life's work with a bittersweet critique of science and technology. While modem science is to be praised for its debunking of the reigning metaphysics - rationalism and its accompanying idealism - it does not emerge unscathed by criticism. At the end of his life his concern is for the mechanistic relationship between mind and reality, endorsed by an increasingly technocratic society: science and technology continue to facilitate the operation and management of objects through mechanization, the subject as living, thinking, creating being retreats into quasi-anonymity. Science "impoverishes" (Gaudin, 155) the subject by rendering him secondary to the automatic functioning of reality. Objects, such as light switches or buttons, are mere instruments in an automated chain of reactions before which the human subject is passive and "dehumanized" (155). As science's domain becomes more expansive, as knowledge strives toward 'absolute' truth, the subject loses much of the very subjectivity which generated the initial quest for knowledge.

What Bachelard is advocating, however, is not an edenic return to prehistory. The industrial and technological operation that science has set in motion cannot be reversed. What he does propose is an enlightened science which elects poetry as its helmsman. Poetry boasts a "prowess of language" that is able to exhume "possibilities" (156) within objects themselves, and "restores" (156) us to the object which has been "caught and crystallized" (Gaudin, 156) by a technocratic society. Objects are more than items to be utilized for efficient ends. When we view them through the lens of the poetic image, they become illuminated by the interplay of word and being, or what Bachelard calls the "iridescent...shimmering...endless..." (in Gaudin, 157) duality of subject and object. We cannot surrender the cultural baggage of science any more than we can strip civilization of its literature, history or social mores. But we can reinvest in objects their "human values" (Bachelard, La Flamme d'une chandelle, 89-94) - those qualities that technology has snuffed out in the name of utility.

Bachelard's celebrated ode to a forgotten lamp is curiously reminiscent of the anthropomorphic tendencies of vitalism and animism. While the text pays an appropriate respect to the "utensility" (FC, 89-94) of the lamp - its function in providing light - it gives at least equal homage to its "seductiveness" (89-94). Bachelard alludes to Henri Bosco's childhood memories of lamplight and the images of solace and companionship it offered:

> We soon realize, and not without emotion, that the lamp is someone. By day, we thought it was just something to be used. But when daylight fades and we find ourselves in a lonely house

> where gathering shadows mean that we must feel our way alongthe wall if we are to move, then we go in search of the lamp we cannot find, only to discover it in a place we had forgotten; the lamp we have found at last and that our hands now closely grasp offers us its gentle, reassuring presence, even before it is lit. It brings us peace of mind, it thinks of us.... [118]

Bachelard's praise of memory and its evocative power to rekindle the "first poetic realities" (89-94) that childhood discovers recalls Proust's "remembrance" of indelible sensations that seem to still the flurry of lost time. Just as the dipped tea cake unfurled a host of forgotten impressions, so poetic sensitivity "deepen(s) the fellowship that we enjoy with kindly objects" (89-94) and untaps the "forces of light that are locked in the prison house of matter" (89-94).

The authentic being of objects lies neither in the taxonomy of concepts that identify them, nor in the sur-rational scope of the new scientific mind. Poetry alone can "nourish" (FC, pp. 4, 56) the reader by removing him from the "cruelly stark" (Gaudin, 161) dimension of everyday language and experience. The poetic word is iconoclastic, breaking with "common sense... (and its) slumbering ...habits of seeing and speaking" (FC, 72). Only through the transubstantiating power of poetry can we rediscover our "verticality,"[119] and in so doing recall our birthright: the "linguistic space

---
118 Bachelard's footnote, Henri Bosco, "Un oublie moins profond," trans Colette Gaudin, Paris: Gallimard, 1961, p. 316.
119 Bachelard's symbol for "our progress, ... our human being." Gaudin, p. 161.

(Bachelard, La Poetique de l'espace, (Paris: P.U.F., 1957), p. 11)" in which we dwell:

> Everything that is specifically human in man is logos; we can never manage to meditate in an area that exists before language.[120]

For Bachelard, our acknowledgment of the autonomy of language is a liberating phenomenon that guarantees the "dialectic of meaning and possibility within each word" (Gaudin, 163). Our origin in language, far from restricting our freedom, prevents 'things themselves' from establishing their tyranny over words.

Bachelard imagines the subject-object structure as a "spiral" (PE, 193) that unfixes meaning by redefining the boundaries between words and things. Man is a "half-open being, on the surface which separates the region of the same from the region of the other" (PE, 199-200). Truth is the symbiosis of mind and world, a helix of "closure and openness" (Gaudin, 163) that takes its cue from language. Poetry, by detaching words from their habitual associations, rejuvenates and "unfixes language" (Gaudin, 163), restoring to it the polyvalence that was its original task in "living the unlived" (163).

Science, by bracketing lived experience, likewise applies reason in the name of a new reality that is as unlived as the imaginary world of poetry. If science is continually enriched by the "pedagogy of ambiguity" (NES, 19) that

---

[120] Bachelard, La Poetique de l'espace, p. 7.

wave mechanics and quantum physics have inaugurated; and if poetry is

continually invigorated by the "pedagogy of the imagination" (Bachelard, Lautreamont, 155) that cures language of its "ankylosis" (NES, 43, PN, 104)"[121], then the mind is free to "cultivate difference" (Gaudin, 169). Bachelard, as we have seen, categorically denies the notion of a monolithic absolute (e.g., transcendental signifier, ultimate particle, final theory), subject to which differences are leveled by a triumvirate of "clarity, coherence, consistency" (Gaudin, 168). In response to the metaphysics of homogeneity that modern thought has inherited, Bachelard insists on the urgency of erecting a new metaphysics - one that is receptive to the malleability of the new scientific mind and the psycho-mythical imagination of modern poetry. Yet even more subversive is Bachelard's blurring of the jurisdictions of poetry and science. In Le Nouvel Esprit scientifique he praises the "poetic strivings of mathematicians" (35); at a Prague conference he compares chemistry to poetry, announcing that "some chemical bodies created by man are no more real than the Aeneid or the Divine Comedy" (Etudes..., 83); in Lautreamont he suggests that certain poems might best be understood as "independent systems just as non-Euclidean geometry is understood as having its own axiomatics" (97). By mathematizing poetry and making science poetic, Bachelard dispels the either-or exclusivity of rationalism and delights in the creative indecidability of

---

121 Bachelard refers to "ankylosis" as a "psychological hardening" that thrives on reason and clarity, the passing on of accepted ideas, and the deference to traditional academic values. (NES, p. 87 and AS, p. 278).

'both-and'. By challenging the comfortable notion of an immutable, sovereign subject that conforms to the "a priori...traditional reason of philosophers" (Gaudin, 170), Bachelard considers the possibility of a "nonfounding reason and a nonfounding subject" (170) - a dialectical absolute that is neither entirely rational nor completely imaginary.

While Bachelard questions the unchallenged dichotomies of philosophy, he likewise offers a new perspective on the role of failure in the scientific method. Error is not to be regarded simply as a wandering of the rational mind away from a singular path toward absolute truth; rather it is to be approached as "...a new fact, a new idea" (ER, 39) — a strident reminder that knowledge is never complete. Failure to grasp a difficult concept, far from discouraging success, should be welcomed as an inauguration of "newness, of openness" (Gaudin, 172). With each failed attempt at understanding, the mind is confronted with a "resistant, unknowable, inexhaustible reality" [122] and is led to an awareness of its own fundamental incompleteness. Ironically, it is our scientific investigation of nature that brings us to an understanding of truth that is unmistakably meta-physical ('beyond nature'). By accepting the unknown, the unfinished, the undisclosed, we as intellectual beings experience - albeit not without some reluctance - the sense of "being bound to something beyond ourselves... "(Gaudin, 172). Bachelard redefines error as an

[122] Jones, p. 18.

occasion for human growth, progress and self-discovery; he rallies for a new humanism that thrives not on "completeness...coherence and control" (173) but on the demystification of the subject's presumptuous mastery of truth.

In dethroning the subject of traditional humanism, Bachelard does not set out to deprive the subject of its natural impetus for transcendence and verticality; knowledge, he claims, will always propel the mind "beyond ordinary experience, beyond nature itself" (Bachelard, Le Materialisme rationnel, pp. 1-2). Thinking - whether it is poetic or scientific - is a way of soliciting a dialogue with reality, of "provok(ing) the world by the instrument of reason and imagination" (Bachelard, ARPC, 141, in Gaudin, 175). Both poetry and science advocate the subject's emergent, problematic posture vis-a-vis reality. The effort of the mind's cryptic path toward truth - whether it be in the *"chiaroscuro* of a dreamer's mind" (FC, 111-12) or in the "constructive difficulties of modern science" (Gaudin, 176) - constitutes "the greatest possible existence" (FC, 111-12) for man. In each frustrated attempt, the subject is "pulled forward and forward again to something beyond, to something above" (111-12) and is reminded of his need for transcendence, his search for an absolute that is both "more-than-being" (111-12) and less than the Being of metaphysics.

CHAPTER NINETEEN: SCIENCE AND POETRY

The reader is understandably perplexed by Bachelard's two vastly different conceptions of the new absolute. On the one hand, he invokes the quaternary[123] forms of the material imagination, as the 'reve-lation' of absolute truth; on the other hand, he returns like the prodigal son to the rigors of science, fueled by reason, where he hopes that a hyper-rational "cogito" can mimic absolute transcendence. It is his ambitious endeavor to "make poetry and science complementary, to unite them as two well-defined opposites"(PF, 2) that becomes the subject of La Formation de l'esprit scientifique and The Psychoanalysis of Fire, published in 1937 and 1938, respectively. The free play of imagination, which both science and poetry exploit, provides a meeting ground for their eventual accord, while at the same time preventing reason's degeneration under the "utilitarian prejudice of pragmatism" (Smith, 75).

In The Psychoanalysis of Fire Bachelard locates the psychological source of literary images in their material bases; it is from this correlation that he claims a "classification of objective themes... [and] poetic temperaments" (PF, 89) may be composed. The four primary physical elements - fire, water, air and **earth - correspond to four "categories of souls" (PF, 89) that in turn**

---
[123] The four forms of the imagination: air, water, earth, fire.

determine the imaginative meaning and style of a work. As fundamental images that anchor a literary text, these four elements are poetry's gateway to the truth of being. While here Bachelard may seem to betray science by condoning a metaphysics of substance, he is in effect declaring that the new ontological status of the aesthetic does not preclude a concurrent search for truth. Reason and imagination are separate poles of the psyche that may work synergistically: the mind can surrender to the "ontological temptation of beauty without abandoning" (Smith, 77) the quest for knowledge.

With the publication of Lautreamont, Bachelard seems to find a peaceful resolution of his frustrated ambivalence toward the epistemological findings of science and the ontological fruits of the literary imagination. What he calls "lautreamontism" (L, 155-56) is none other than the literary corollary to science's 'rupture' with immediate perception. Bachelard heralds both poetry and science as two avenues to a new "dialectical transcendence" (Smith, 81) that can creatively accommodate the essentialism of metaphysics and Jungian psychology, and the subjectivism of modern science. Faith in the eternal truth of literary images and "symbolic reality" (Smith, 80) is not incompatible, *ipso facto,* with relativity and its cynical treatment of absolute knowledge. Bachelard's comparison of projective geometry with Lautreamont's "projective poetry" (L 54) confirms Les Chants de Maldoror as an imaginary escape from "the yoke of description" (Smith, 81); like non-Euclidean geometry, projective poetry "violat(es) reality" (Smith, 81) by expanding certain "clusters of images" (81) beyond their hackneyed referents.

L'Eau et les reves (1942) continues Bachelard's tenuous application of the principles of psychoanalysis to the explication of literary texts. Images are "reducible" (Smith, 83) to the four material cornerstones of the imagination which underlie repressed (psychic) complexes. For Bachelard, poetic language is not a replicate of reality; it does not merely transpose visual forms into "imitative literary images" (Smith, 84). "Beyond the images of form," promises Bachelard, "...there are...images of matter, direct images of matter" (Smith, 84). Words are intrinsically associated with archetypes that bear little or no resemblance to their perceptual counterparts. As prototypes of poetic form, these material images constitute an *a priori* of the imagination—an "unconsciousness of form" (ER, 70)—that lends truth and substance to external reality.[124] The image cannot be empirically verified; its "direct apprehension of immediate reality" (Smith, 86) is logically prior to rational thought. Thus, the very specter of metaphysics that Bachelard had rejected in his epistemology is now reintroduced into the realm of literary imagination, where "the real phantom of our imaginary nature...the truth of our being" (ER, 249) resides.

---

124 While both formal imagination and philosophical realism describe the "external qualities" of objects, material imagination uncovers images of "underlying substance" (Smith, p. 85).

In L'Air et les songes (1943) Bachelard offers a more compelling attempt to establish an ontological "ground" (Smith, 91) for literary theory. In one of the most unabashed declarations of his allegiance to Romantic idealism, he claims that it is "air" that is the privileged mouthpiece of truth. Images of air conjure "the means by which we *escape from the real...* (italics mine) (to our) innermost reality" (AS, 14). Aerial images, notes Bachelard, elicit corresponding images of ascension and sublimation. In dreams of flight, for example, images of wings are "rationalizations" (AS, 36) of the impulse of the human will in its ascent toward "inner being" (Smith, 95). Ironically, one does not liberate inner being by descending to psychological or sexual depths, but by rising up to "participate...in being" (AS, 90). Whereas for Freudian psychoanalysis a well-adjusted psyche is one that is monitored by the "reality function" (Smith, 96), for Bachelard the self reaches its fulfillment when it pays equal homage to the unreal:

> ... (A) person deprived of the unreality function is as much of a neurotic as a person deprived of the reality function.[125]

Bachelard insists on the primacy of subjectivity--"the dream before the reality" (AS, 119)-over objectivity. In both science and poetry, it is the reasoning or imagining "spirit" (Smith, 97)--the unreal--which structures given reality and

---
[125] Bachelard, L'Air et les songes, p. 14.

therefore vitiates the supremacy of an a priori absolute.

Notwithstanding modern science's claims to ultimate truth, it is art – in the voice of the poetic word - that is uniquely qualified to imagine "the ineffable, the evasive, the aerial..."(AS, 301-302). For Bachelard, neither idealism nor realism can capture the "exuberance" (AS, 301-302) of emergent truth.[126] The Bachelardian absolute is suspended between the "vertical axis" (Smith, 99) of the imagination and the "horizontal" (99) syntax of reason and discourse. The literary image, for Bachelard, crystallizes the dual movement of "expansion... (and) depth" (AS, 301-302) that is the hallmark of a new, dialectical absolute.

---

[126] As Smith explains, "....Being cannot be limited to external reality, to that which can be conceptually designated." (Smith, p. 90)

PART III

SEARCH FOR A FINAL THEORY

CHAPTER TWENTY: Order Out of Chaos

Both Bachelard and Kristeva are representative of classical disciplines on the brink of self-criticism and renewal. Bachelard asks philosophy of science to reformulate its categories of "objective" knowledge and "absolute" truth. He looks to poetry for an illumination of the truth about the aesthetic and its seminal role in the new concept of scientific objectivity. Kristeva brings literary theory and psychology together in an interdisciplinary endeavor to determine the meaning of the absolute in the modem era.

Modern science is no less baffled by the conundrum of absolute truth, no less driven by a desire to make it the final piece in its "Theory of Everything".[127] For the classical physicist, in the beginning was the "Word" of mathematics, whose quest for the truth about the universe is founded on the immutable laws of reason. The modem scientist, true to the legacy of Kristeva and Bachelard, challenges the limits of reason, exhausting its conceptual framework until he reaches an intellectual impasse. It is at this point that science adopts one of two credos: a decidedly unscientific Sartrean absurdity (i.e., existence is purely contingent) or a mystical belief in a quasi-divine transcendence that takes over where science ends.

---

[127] Theory of Everything is physics' version of the Absolute: a unified, mathematical "...description of the world in terms of a closed system...." (Paul Davies, The Mind of God. (New York: Simon and Schuster, 1992), p. 21.

Science either denies the question of the Absolute as a valid subject for scientific inquiry, or blindly forges ahead in the hopes that Reason may someday propose the final theory to end all mysteries. Some, like science critic John Horgan, vehemently reject the notion that reason has already said all there is to say about the universe. The God of metaphysics may be dead but there will never be an "end" for science.[128] Even though science is closer than ever to the unified theory that physicist Stephen Hawking has likened to knowing the "mind of God"[129], it is hard-pressed to lay claims to ultimate truth. For, each answer begs another question: each "complete theory"[130] touted by physics raises the corpse of metaphysics. I shall examine this intellectual foment in light of Julia Kristeva's inquiry into the absolute through the art of literary theory and the science of psychoanalysis, and in light of Gaston Bachelard's *mise en abime* of the problem of the Absolute vis-a-vis poetry and science.

The search for a final theory has become the secular "holy grail" (Paul Davies, The Mind of God, New York: Simon & Schuster, 1992), p. 21) of modern physics. With the eureka of every new theory that sheds light on the cosmos and man's place in it, science admits the paucity of its own endeavor:

---

[128] John Horgan. The End of Science. London: Little, Brown & Company, 1996.

[129] Stephen Hawking. A Brief History of Time. New York: Bantam Books, 1988, concluding passage.

[130] Hawking, concluding passage.

> In exploring the frontiers of reason and rationality we will certainly encounter mystery and uncertainty and in all probability at some stage reasoning will fail us and have to be replaced either by irrational belief or frank agnosticism.[131]

An unlikely antidote to the failings of reason is the imaginative play that modern scientific theory invokes, often long before empirical verification is plausible. Whereas deductive and inductive reasoning have been the cornerstones of the scientific endeavor, most of the significant advances in modern physics are the result of "free-ranging imaginative...inspiration" (Davies, 28). Scientists are at a loss to explain the gratuitousness of seemingly revelatory flashes of understanding that transcend the bounds of reason. Scientific hubris is kept in check by the indisputable workings of the irrational and the imaginary -- the accomplice and at times the Muse of scientific inquiry.

For Isaac Newton and his contemporaries, the cosmos was a "vast and magnificent machine constructed by God" (Davies, 76) and permeated throughout by fixed mathematical laws that mirrored divine rationality. The hegemony of Reason, with God as its guarantor, gave to science in the classical age the privilege of "uncovering the hidden order...the cosmic code" (Heinz Pagels, The Cosmic Code, (New York: Bantam Books, 1982).

---
[131] Paul Davies, The Mind of God, p. 25.

Modern physics has been stripped of its divine underpinnings and must fashion its own epistemological rationale. Thus the question of final truth is an open-ended one: either the laws of physics are incremental "approximations to a unique set of "true" laws" - the modern-day Platonic Forms - which may someday be known [132] : or, as James Hartle maintains, there is no "single set of rules by which the universe is run with an actuality apart from this world they govern (James Hartle, "Excess Baggage," <u>Particle Physics and the Universe: Essays in Honour of Gell-Mann).</u>

The question of ultimate truth and its accessibility to human understanding is further complicated by the advent of "virtual reality." The increasing self-sufficiency of computers in the simulation of actual beings and events begs the question of whether truth lies beyond the scope of abstract reasoning. If we are caught in an algorithmic web of computer mimesis, then reality is back as the ever-elusive thing-in-itself of Kantian lore. Physicist Frank Tipler has even gone so far as to suggest that science dispense with such vain notions of ultimate reality and a "physically real universe." In order to be empirically pure, he advises, science must restrict itself to the phenomenal world of abstract programs. (Barrow, J.D. and F.J. Tipler)

Post-modern literature has put paid to the notion of the "transcendental signifier"; the social sciences proclaim truth to be a curious admixture of mind

---

[132] This is the opinion of many theoretical physicists, among them Stephen Hawing, whose inaugural lecture for the Lucasian Chair at Cambridge was entitled, "Is the End in Sight for Theoretical Physics?"

and body, semiotic and symbolic, unconscious and conscious; physics is increasingly wary of an empirically verifiable absolute. Yet the very fact that both literature and science continue to theorize belies a faith in a noumenal 'something else,' irreducible to the contingent world of becoming. If science were nothing but a cataloguing of observed results, an inscription of experimental data, the scientific endeavor would have long ago stagnated. If literature were none other than the narrative voice of non-truth, it would have already lost its allure. And if literary criticism did nothing but announce the impotency of literature, it would have long since perished. Scientists and philosophers of science continue to spin theories that attempt to explain the 'why' of the phenomenal world, often in the absence of empirical data. Imagination flies in the face of reason when the scientist asks "what are the "laws of initial conditions" that are "out there", transcending the physical universe" (Davies, 91)? If physics was born with the Big Bang, what were those "meta"-physical determinations that gave birth to the physical world? The fact that there are physicists that frame this type of question in quasi-metaphysical terms re-validates an abstraction that modernity has dismissed as inappropriately animistic and teleological: the absolute.

The underlying premise of modern science is the belief that "the Universe is algorithmically compressible" (Davies, 136); i.e., there are unifying principles, or laws, that synthesize in a meaningful way the contingent facts of reality.

Without this foundation, writes Barrow, "all science would be replaced by mindless stamp collecting - the indiscriminate accumulation of every available fact" (John Barrow, Theories of Everything: The Quest for Ultimate Explanations, (Oxford: Clarendon Press, 1991), p. 11). This prejudice, however, reaches certain limits when forced to make sense of data that do not conform to traditional standards of lawful behavior - e.g., random, chaotic events. Reminiscent of the "unnamable" truth of the Kristevan Sublime and the evanescent "verticality" of the Bachelardian absolute, chaos does not fit neatly into the predictable categories of space and time. [133] Yet, rather than dismiss such randomness as unknowable or irrational, scientists recognize its power to exhibit a logic of a different kind. Chaotic events, they claim, while devoid of "regimented regularity" (Davies, 139), nevertheless display order. Such "organized complexity" (139) possesses a rational "depth" that is not immediately observable but which, only after great effort and difficulty, yields patterns of great meaning. Whereas Newtonian science uncovered the gross patterns that governed physical phenomena, post-modern science demands that those laws be malleable enough to account for "deep systems" (138)- e.g., human free will and biological structures - which display a value that is highly complex, algorithmically.

---

[133] Some examples of chaotic systems are: turbulent fluids, dripping taps, fibrillating hearts. Paul Davies, p. 136.

When seeking order in classical physics, in random systems, or in quantum probability, scientists differ in their qualification of the role they attribute to mathematics. Physicist Eugene Aligner has spoken of the "unreasonable effectiveness of mathematics...;"[134] there are those that go so far as to posit a "deep and meaningful significance behind nature's mathematical face" (Davies, 140). There are scientists of the Platonic school that endow mathematical concepts with a transcendent existence that the mind can discover; and there are those who deny a "timeless, absolute" (140) mathematics, seeing it only as a clever human invention that matches the facts of experience. Two of the most celebrated contemporary mathematicians—Kurt Godel and Roger Penrose—are self-proclaimed essentialists. Both admit that, while it is customary to assume that mathematics is a largely if not completely formalistic activity, it is nevertheless almost impossible not to resist the belief that certain elements, like the system of complex numbers, have a "profound and timeless reality."[135] Godel's theory of "undecidability" argues that, since there will always be mathematical statements that are true but can never be "proved to be true from existing axioms" (Davies, 142), these true statements must exist a priori, "out there" (142). Likewise, Oxford mathematician Roger Penrose maintains that mathematical truth far

---

[134] Eugene Wagner. Communications in Pure and Applied Mathematics 13. 1960, p. 1.
[135] Roger Penrose. The Emperor's New Mind: Conerning Computers, Minds and the Laws of Physics. Oxford University Press: Oxford, 1989, p. 111.

surpasses the boundaries of formalism:

> There often does appear to be some profound...reality about these mathematical concepts, going quite beyond the deliberations of any particular mathematician. It is as though human thought is, instead, being guided towards some *eternal, external truth* (italics mine) - a Truth which has a reality of its own....[136]

Yet another example of the universality of mathematics is the "Mandelbrot set", named after the computer scientist Benoit Mandelbrot. Simply put, the set is a complex pattern generated by "successive applications of the ...rule (z, where z squared plus c)..."(Davies, 142) which when plotted as dots on a graph form random groupings. Out of a radically simple input function emerges an "extraordinarily complicated structure" (143) whose beauty and diversity cannot be accounted for by any logical (i.e, algorithmic) means. Mandelbrot himself, it is said, was unaware of the latent complexity of his set. As Penrose remarks,

> The complete details of the complication of the structure of Mandelbrot's set cannot really be fully comprehended by any one of us, nor can it be fully revealed by any computer. It would seem that this structure is not just part of our minds, but it has a reality of its own...The Mandelbrot set is not an invention of the human mind: it was a discovery. Like Mount Everest, the Mandelbrot set is just there.[137]

---
136 Ibid., p. 111.
137 Ibid., p. 111.

Penrose regards such eternal truths as the Mandelbrot set rather like glimpses of a divine transcendence, in much the same way that pantheistic philosophies explain the physical world as the natural emanation of a Supreme Being.

Roger Penrose ascribes to the idealist notion of mathematical forms that are accessible through the medium of thought alone. The immediacy of this transcendent world of ideas guarantees the communion of minds; for each mathematician has a "direct route to truth" and each is "directly in contact with the same eternally existing Platonic world" (Penrose, 428) The shocking, revelatory nature of these intuitions of mathematical truth is reported by mathematician Carl Gauss; after years of grappling with a mathematical riddle, Gauss recalls, "...like a...flash of lightning, the riddle happened to be solved."[138] In the same fortuitous manner, scientist Henri Poincare reflects on the Proustian nature of his encounter with mathematical truth: "At the moment when I put my foot on the step, the idea came to me, without anything in my former thoughts seeming to have paved the way for it."[139] Penrose recalls a similar mystical experience while working on a theory of black holes and space-time irregularities. The moment of recognition or truth

---
[138] Jacques Hadamard. The Psychology of Invention in the Mathematical Field. Princeton: Princeton University Press, 1949, p. 13.
[139] Ibid., p. 12.

appeared first as a fleeting idea that he almost dismissed as trivial; only later when he became aware of a "curious feeling of elation....he remembered the brief inspirational flash, and knew it was the key to the problem... "(Davies, 145). Far removed from the linearity of inductive reasoning and experiment, mathematical inspiration is anchored by an intuitive grasp of truth, inexplicably irrupting ideas, equally irrational recollections of truth, and finally the conversion of raw, revealed truth into concept and theory.

On the opposite side of the intellectual spectrum are mainstream computer scientists who maintain that "what can't be computed is meaningless" (Davies, 146). Rolf Landauer is a proponent of the viewpoint that, ultimately, computers will determine the lawfulness of physics. Unless the laws of physics - nothing but "algorithms for the processing of information," he claims - are applicable to our universe, they are meaningless.[140] And if mathematics and physics are human constructs that are by definition bound by space, time, and history, then speculations as to the origin of the universe and its absolute truth are no longer valid. Somewhere in between Penrose the Platonist and Landauer the formalist lies the viewpoint of mathematicians James Jeans and G.H. Hardy. While mathematical truth, they argue, may not

---
[140] Rolf Landauer, "Computation and Physics: Wheeler's Meaning Circuit?" Foundations of Physics 16. 1986, p. 551.

be 'out there' to discover, and while the human mind may indeed impose its mathematical constructs on a neutral world, there is nevertheless reason to believe that science does "uncover some real property of nature" (Davies, 151). Penrose takes their realism one step further, insisting that there must be ...some deep underlying reason for the accord between mathematics and physics" (Penrose, 430); for the theories that stand the test of time are simply too 'truthful' to be the result of chance or contingency.

The acceptance of quantum mechanics as one of the "astonishing" (Davies, 152) theories whose success cannot be defined by purely formal criteria begs the question of how science can accept as 'absolutely' true a theory whose very essence is uncertainty. Is physics conceding the irony that the only eternal truths - relativity and quantum mechanics - yield no truth at all, just "fuzziness....smearing out the values of all observable quantities in an unpredictable way" (Davies, 158)? Many scientists entertain the idea that quantum undecidability leaves room for an element of mystery and as such is a more truthful paradigm than the classical "closed system", in which "everything is accounted for and no mystery remains" (Davies, 161-162). Others hope that even those laws of physics which are deemed to be immutable may yet be reintegrated into a "completely unifying superlaw"

(Davies, 164). Oxford chemist Peter Atkins argues that the apparent "convergence" of physics toward an overriding Uber-law validates the theory that the physical world is the way it is "necessarily" (Davies, 164). If this evolution toward a progressively unified theory converges in a "totally unified account of all the laws of nature" (165), then the philosophical quest for the Absolute may come to rest in a Theory of Everything.

In <u>Theories of Everything: The Quest for Ultimate Explanation,</u> John Barrow attributes the confidence in elaborating a final theory to an historical tradition that crystallized in the Enlightenment premise that the universe is rationally knowable. The fundamental belief that "...there is a graspable logic behind physical existence that can be compressed into a compelling and succinct form" (Davies, 165)- i.e., mathematical theory – is the energy that drives the quest for absolute meaning. This faith, however, is not without its cynics and critics. Russell Stannard is among those scientists for whom a unification of physics is a vain and illusory goal. How, Stannard challenges, can one theory feasibly explain not only the origin of the universe, but why only one set of laws suffices to explain it exhaustively?

> ... (An) inherent, unavoidable lack of completeness must reflect itself in whatever mathematical system models our universe. As creatures belonging to the physical world, we will be included as part of that model. It follows that we shall never be able to justify the choice of axioms

in the model.....Nor shall we be able to account for all true statements that can be made about the universe.' [141]

Barrow is equally cynical about totalizing theories that lay claims to absolute truth. The limitations drawn by Godel's theory of incompleteness, he observes, would make suspect any theory aspiring to account for everything. It would be unlikely at best, Barrow believes, that such a theory could adequately incorporate all the complexity of the universe:

> There is no formula that can deliver all truth, all harmony, all simplicity. No Theory of Everything can ever provide total insight. For, to see through everything would leave us seeing nothing at all.[142]

Barrow's dismissal of an absolute theory leaves room for an implicit acknowledgement of the Unknown. By denying that science, or reason, can ever hope to attain an adequate Theory of Everything, he unwittingly endows the Absolute with more metaphysical properties than most scientists would admit. Mystery, the infinite, the unknown - all are categories usually reserved for philosophers and theologians in their depictions of Being or God. Like Barrow, philosopher Thomas Torrance reminds scientists that

---
[141] Russell Stannard, "No Faith in the Grand Theory," The Times. London, 13 November, 1989.
[142] John Barrow. Theories of Everything: the Quest for Ultimate Explanation. Oxford: Clarendon Press, 1991, p. 40.

> ...there is no intrinsic reason in the universe why it should exist at all, or why it should be what it actually is: hence we deceive ourselves if in our natural science we think we can establish that the universe could only be what it is.[143]

What incites even the most positivistic of scientists to consider the task of pursuing a final theory is the impasse that, like it or not, every physicist will have to confront; namely, "Why does the universe go to all the bother of existing? What is it that breathes fire into the equations and makes a universe for them to describe?"[144]

Despite the persistent faith in science's ability to arrive at a unifying theory that satisfies the principle of sufficient reason,[145] most physicists and mathematicians admit the unlikelihood of such an enterprise. Ultimately, science may be compelled to look for rational explanations "in something beyond or outside the physical world - in something metaphysical ..." because a contingent universe (one that is characterized by becoming, complexity and chaos, as well as lawful order and predictability) by definition excludes its own explanatory principle.

---

[143] Thomas Torrance. Divine and Contingent Order. Oxford: Oxford University Press. 1981, p. 36.
[144] Stephen Hawking. A Brief History of Time. London and New York: Bantam, 1988, p. 174.
[145] i.e., the principle that the world is rational and intelligible, and that everything "is as it is for some reason." Davies, p. 162.

Ironically, the physicists who are most committed to the Arthurian search for a unifying theory are those who, prima facie, appear to be the most distanced from mathematical physics - specifically, those scientists who apply aesthetic standards to physics' search for truth. It is a widely held belief among such scientists that "beauty is a reliable guide to truth, and (that significant)...advances in theoretical physics have been made by...demanding mathematical elegance of a new theory" (Davies, 175). Aesthetics as an epistemological method, however, brings with it the accompanying baggage of subjectivity and relativism. How can the finality of a unifying theory of the universe be judged by such a mutable criterion as beauty, for which there is no objective barometer? Absent a universal measurement for beauty, is not each emergent final theory relative to the aesthetic prejudice of the scientist? Simply put, each Theory of Everything is merely a theory of Someone; for "... there are all sorts of biological and psychological factors at work in framing our impressions of what is beautiful" (Davies, 176). One solution to the relativist dilemma is offered by Paul Davies, who aligns himself with Roger Penrose's platonic model of mathematical and aesthetic forms. He believes that a comprehensive model of 'essential' Beauty is the source of our "aesthetic appreciation" (Davies, 176) and that science, as well as art and literature, can come into contact with this " "something" ...firmer and more pervasive" (176).... For Penrose, the impulse to know and the seemingly gratuitous recognition of certain immutable laws both derive from "aesthetic convictions.....Rigorous argument is usually the last step" (Penrose, 421)!

Just as Bachelard grappled with the dichotomy of theory and imagination, and as Kristeva elaborated the doublebind of the symbolic and the semiotic, modern science is faced with the dilemma of how to reconcile immutable physical laws with a universe of contingent becoming. One of the more prominent paradigms for reconciling this dualism is adapted from "process thought" - an offspring of theology introduced by mathematician and philosopher Alfred North Whitehead. According to Whiteheadian physics, experience is a "network... (linking) actual occasions" (in Davies, 183). Unlike the physical events of Newtonian physics, "actual occasions" have an intentionality and freedom that constitute reality as an unpredictable process a constant process of becoming. God intervenes as "participator in the creative" (Davies, 183) event, guiding it toward a teleological resolution (i.e., Absolute). Yet the essential openness and indeterminacy of the universe is intact, no longer predestined by an omniscient Creator. In this way, process philosophy is able to situate the Absolute within the process itself of chance and becoming, from which it has been traditionally estranged, and propose a rather unorthodox metaphysics that is compatible with uncertainty and change.

The theistic model may be the only "simplifying and unifying description" (Davies, 189) that is able to coordinate the stringent laws of physics with the human spirit's imaginative longing for its own role in absolute truth. Once the laws of physics have been applied exhaustively, the "brute fact" of existence and its pure contingency become apparent. Philosopher Richard Swinburne claims that human beings find it unbearable to accept the idea of a universe that is 'just there'; Davies and others like him find it more reasonable, and more consoling, to "posit the existence of an infinite mind" (Horgan, 188) in which even such chaotic structures as "stochastic systems" maintain their integrity. As open structures that are subject to random fluctuations - instability, atomic events, etc - and which are free to "explore genuine novelty" (192), stochastic systems pose a challenge to teleological systems. Yet, as Davies asserts, the apparent absurdity of an isolated quantum event often exhibits an ordered pattern when observed as part of an "ensemble" (Davies, 193). And as physicist John Wheeler has noted, patterned behavior or characteristics are often derived from chaos and random fluctuations. God may be, as Whitehead speculated, that higher force that coaxes disordered, irrational events toward a reasonable whole.

CHAPTER TWENTY-ONE: SACRED SCIENCE

Perhaps modern science's failure to conceptualize a "Theory of Everything" is a statement about the nature of knowledge itself. In looking for the final truth of the universe, science may have to broaden its epistemological tools to include not only aesthetics, as Davies and Penrose have suggested, but "intellection" (Nasr, 23) and revelation. Scholar of "traditional studies" Seyyed Hossein Nasr, in his address given in New Delhi commemorating the 60th birthday of the Dalai Lama, condemns the degeneration of what was once a holistic *scientia sacra* into a pagan science of nature. Modern science, rather than respecting the boundaries of empirical knowledge, has absolutized scientific knowledge, endowing it with the prerogative of subjugating nature to its whim. In legitimizing and empowering science as the excusive domain of knowledge, Nasr argues, Western culture denies itself the wisdom that is earned from "contemplation of [the] ontological and symbolic reality" (Nasr, 24) of the universe. The scientific endeavor, he explains, must comprise much more than the "systematic knowledge of nature, combined with mathematics" (25) which burgeoned in the Scientific Revolution of the 17th century. It must also pursue the sacred aspect of reality - its spiritual dimension that is, Nasr claims, "beyond mental categories but is *not anti-intellectual (*italics mine), Nasr, 27)".

Knowledge of the Absolute, or the sacred, dispenses with the conceptual categories of the mind and activates a "divine noetic faculty" (28)—the Intellect—whose task is to know that which cannot be empirically verified. The great *faux pas* of modern science is to absolutize[146] the relative - i.e., observable reality—and to insist on solely empirical means of knowing reality. Modern technocratic society, due to the predominance of the scientific world view, accepts the "cosmic illusion" (Nasr, 29) as reality. Only the "psycho-physical, the sensible and the measurable" (29) are deemed sufficiently objective to warrant the approval of modern science:

> Many of (science's) exponents ...set about to reveal the mysteries of existence through the microscope, telescope, or some computer model, and a world dazzled by the glitter of modern technology and having divinized modern science stands with full anticipation for the revelation of the next "mystery of the universe" which does not usually go beyond adding or subtracting some purely quantitative element to or from the universe seen in a purely quantitative manner.[147]

Nasr praises the recent efforts of modern science to converge toward spirituality and to attempt to reconsider the sacred as more than epiphenomenal. While its first attempts may appear contrived, they nevertheless represent a re-valorisation of "...reality in its vast amplitude and numerous dimensions" (36). Modern man must cultivate a sacred science of

---

[146] What Whitehead called "The Fallacy of Misplaced Concreteness... the accidental error of mistaking the abstract for the concrete." Whitehead, Science and the Modern World. New York: Macmillan Publishing Company, Inc., 1925, p. 51

[147] H.S. Nasr, Sophia 1. Oakton, Virginia: The Foundation for Traditional Studies, 1995, p. 29.

the cosmos which would not refute the findings of physics, yet provide a new understanding of the spiritual dimension of the cosmos - one that can peaceably co-exist with science. Modern physics must take its place as one among several possible sciences and not the "...only legitimate science of nature" (39). By falsely attributing ultimate truth to the physical world of science, we repress a multitude of hierarchical levels of reality that span the narrowing gulf between reason and the sacred. Absolute knowledge, far from bracketing spirituality, is based upon the basic tenet "...that not only are there levels of reality but also levels of consciousness which can know those levels of reality" (39).

Despite science's recent, if not reluctant, accommodation of sacred modes of knowing, some scientists persist in the assertion that the universe has been stripped "of all mystery and purpose" (Davies, 195) and that the laws of nature are sufficiently rational to explain the workings of the universe. Physicist Steven Weinberg observes with irony the increasing correlation between the comprehensibility of the universe and its meaninglessness.[148] Biologist Jacques Monod offers a bitter commentary on man's place in a universe without an Absolute, divine or otherwise:

> The ancient covenant is in pieces: man at last knows that he is alone in the unfeeling immensity of the universe, out of which he

---
[148] Steven Weinberg. The First Three Minutes. London: Andre Deutsch, 1977, p. 149.

has emerged only by chance. Neither his destiny nor his duty have been written down.[149]

Without direction or devotion, man is left to comment on the absurd: self-organizing systems of matter and energy that frustrate reason and pose as nature's secular absolute.

As early as the seventeenth century, scientists were remarking on the fortuitous compatibility between the cosmos and living beings. In 1913 Harvard biochemist Lawrence Henderson claimed that the "properties of matter and the course of cosmic evolution" were so inextricably linked to biology as to suggest that the universe might be "in its very essence...biocentric."[150] John Gribbin and Martin Rees, in Cosmic Coincidences, theorize that the conditions of the universe "...really do seem to be uniquely suitable for life forms like ourselves:[151] While most modern scientists try to avoid making conclusions that adhere to the Anthropic Principle, [152] most marvel at the fact that even minute variations in the initial conditions of the universe would render it at best incomprehensible, at worst lifeless. Physicists such as Davies and John Polkinghorne (who left particle physics for the priesthood) call for a continued confidence that a unified

---

[149] Jacques Monod. Chance and Necessity. Trans. A. Wainhouse, London: Collins, 1972, p. 167.
[150] L. J. Henderson. The Fitness of the Environment, reprinted by Peter Smith, Massachusetts, 1970, p. 342.
[151] Religion and the Scientists, ed. Mervyn Stockwook, Londond: SCM, 1959, p. 82.
[152] ....the linkage between human observership and the laws and conditions of the universe. Davies, p. 299.

theory is imminent. Despite the air of desperation among theorists who are committed to an all-embracing theory, all the indications suggest that "...in due course some deeper understanding will be achieved and a more profound pattern discerned at the basis of physical reality." [153]

Yet even if the awe-inspiring beauty and organized complexity that have emerged out of the initial conditions are one day incorporated into some grand scheme, one lingering question will no doubt continue to vex humankind: why this final theory and not some other? Why this universe rather than nothing at all? Skeptics of both theology and theoretical physics maintain that the mutual dependency of observer and observed necessitated by quantum mechanics creates a situation of "observer-participancy" (Davies, 224) that precludes knowledge of eternal laws. John Wheeler, creator of this image of the universe as a "self-excited circuit"[154] that generates itself, argues that it is not only unnecessary but impossible to get outside the loop to question transcendence or immutable laws. Only through observation of physical reality does physical reality come into being; even the laws of physics "must have come into being with the big bang" (Wheeler, p. 8).

Wheeler's closed-loop model, while inventive in its own right, fails on several accounts. Not only is it unable to explain itself, since to do that would

---

[153] John Polkinghorne, "The Faith of a Physicist," Physics Education 22, 1987, p. 12.
[154] John Wheeler, "Information, Physics, Quantum: The Search for Links," Complexity, Entropy, and the Physics of Information, ed. W. Wojciech H. Zurek and Addison-Wesley. Redwood City, California, 1990, p. 8.

require an objective perspective that the theory by definition excludes; but it lacks completeness - it leaves unanswered the question of ―Why that loop?"...or even "Why does any loop exist at all?" (Davies, 225). An exhaustive account of the universe might require an appeal to causal principles that lie "outside the usual categories of rational human thought" (225). For even the most "refined and formalized" (225) of mathematical theorems cannot account for all elements of uncertainty and incompleteness.

Scientific inquiry has yet to provide a conclusive, final theory that adequately answers all of the 'why' questions that lie outside the scope of logical reasoning. There are those scientists, like Stephen Hawking, who are convinced that science may some day come to explore the "mind of God" -- that mathematical reasoning may progress sufficiently to be able to conceptualize the Absolute. Still others deny that reason can ever get outside its own conceptual apparatus to theorize the irrational; only an imaginative or spiritual mode of knowing is able to bring the mind into contact with ultimate reality. Among the latter group, those who adhere to some form of mysticism are the most adamantly opposed to logical reasoning as an inroad to absolute truth. Russell Stannard recalls his own mystical encounter with an omnipotent power of some kind; it is, he claims, "...of a nature to command respect and awe....There is a sense of urgency about it; the power is volcanic...." [155] For philosopher of science David Peat, the revelation of the Absolute seems to cloak the world in a profound meaning that rational thought could only hope to attain:

> We sense that we are touching something universal and perhaps eternal, so that the particular moment in time takes on a numinous character and seems to expand in time without limit. We sense that all boundaries between ourselves and the outer world vanish, for what we are experiencing lies *beyond all categories and all attempts to be captured in logical thought* (italics mine) .[156]

Mathematician Rudy Rucker is convinced that a mystical encounter is the only means of approximating a 'knowledge' of the Absolute. While science may be able to snatch glimpses of truth over time, "no door in the labyrinthine castle of science opens directly onto the Absolute." [157] Godel himself was able to adopt a different stance to reality through meditation: by relinquishing the categories of mathematical reasoning and logic, he could come into direct, unmediated contact with such unobservable objects as infinity. Davies rejects the existentialist convictions of those scientists who are "...opposed temperamentally to any form of metaphysical, let alone mystical arguments" (Davies, 231). He reasons that by asking the most perplexing, unanswerable

---
155 Russell Stannard. Grounds for Reasonable Belief. Edinburgh: Scottish Academic Press, 1989, p. 169.
156 David Peat. The Philosopher's Stone: The Sciences of Synchronicity and Creativity. New York: Bantam Doubleday, 1991, on the press.
157 Rudy Rucker. Infinity and the Mind. Boston: Birkhauser, 1987, pp. 47-170.

questions about truth, science is brought to that very threshold where reason and logic collapse. Only at this point, when reason has humbled science to admit that a "closed and complete system of logical truths is almost certainly impossible" (231), is the mind able to construct an epistemological model that might intuit absolute truth.

CHAPTER TWENTY-TWO: BEAUTIFUL DREAMER

According to author and physicist Steven Weinberg, it is with Isaac Newton that "the modern dream of a final theory really begins." [158] Newtonian laws of motion and universal gravitation provided such a comprehensive account of the workings of nature that for the first time science entertained the possibility of absolute knowledge. By 1902, physicists speculated:

> The day appears not far distant when the converging lines from many apparently remote regions of thought will meet on...common ground.... [All] of these will be marshaled into a single and compact body [of scientific knowledge] ....[159]

Yet scientific hubris was soon greeted with the sobering realities of quantum mechanics. Newtonian reductionism and determinism were tempered by the much less ambitious probability theory, in which "humans play an essential role in giving meaning..." (Weinberg, 77). Quantum mechanics seemed to deride the smug predictions of classical physics, all the while tempting the scientist with a "beauty [that is] but a dream" (Weinberg, 17) of the absolute truth that a final theory would unveil. Calculations of probability fail to provide the repose of predictable certainty

---

[158] Steven Weinberg. Dreams of a Final Theory. New York: Vintage Books, 1993.
[159] A. Michelson, "The Day Appears Not Far Distant," Light Waves and Their Uses. Chicago: University of Chicago Press, 1903, p. 163.

that Newtonian physics felt assured of. But the progressively accurate and beautiful "approximations to the truth" (Weinberg, 85) that are the hallmarks of quantum mechanics give a glimpse of a larger, aesthetic truth that is closer to the Bachelardian "connaissance approchee". Those scientists that maintain the feasibility of a final theory believe that quantum mechanics may well be a permanent feature of a "deeper truth" (Weinberg, 89). Einstein himself, when questioned about the truthfulness of relativity, cited the "attractiveness" (Weinberg, 102) of its underlying principles. And for British astronomers, the 'truth' of relativity lay not in its veracity, but rather in the fact that "...it was plausible enough and beautiful enough to be worth devoting a fair fraction of their own research careers to test its predictions... "(Weinberg, 103). Reason and empirical evidence are inextricably tied, in the post-Newtonian model of truth, to aesthetic judgment, imagination, and intuition. The stark simplicity of an aesthetically compelling theory convinces the modern physicist often long before the verification of experimental data.

But simplicity is not the only criterion of truth in post-Newtonian physics; the sense of "inevitability" (Weinberg, 135) of a theory that has explanatory power as well as sheer beauty provides "an intense aesthetic pleasure" (135) analogous to the enjoyment of a timeless work of art. A final theory evokes a sense of eternality and universality that the scientist recognizes as true, simply because it provides the "symmetry" and "rigidity" of a "beautiful explanatory theory" (Weinberg, 148):

> The kind of beauty that we find in physical theories is of a very limited sort. It is...the beauty of perfect structure, the beauty of everything fitting together, of nothing being changeable, of logical rigidity. It is a beauty that is spare and classic, the sort we find in the Greek tragedies.[160]

Ironically, the beauty of these theories and their mathematical structures is so provocative of some deeper truth that the structures prevail even when their underlying principles are disproved. In the late 1920's Dirac's theory of electron spin and subsequent discovery of cosmic rays met with great prestige; we now know that the theory is "largely wrong" (Weinberg, 151), yet the mathematical structures that supported Dirac's theories survive as a vital part of quantum field theory. Thus, while the scientist may be inspired by the physical principles of mathematical structures, their beauty is of a timeless "portability...that survive(s) when the principles themselves do not" (151). Even more extraordinary is the fact that it is often the scientist's intuited sense of beauty that leads him to valid theories, even when that intuition flies in the face of reason. The aesthetic principle, piloted by the imagination, approaches truth where experimental evidence may even prove the contrary (Weinberg, 157).

Reason and empirical evidence still have their all-important roles to play in scientific inquiry. But more and more frequently, "aesthetic judgments" (165)

---
[160] Weinberg, p. 149.

are taking over where rational explanations reach an impasse. Weinberg maintains that, if physics continues to study "fundamental problems" (165)"- questions about the origin of life, final theory, truth-it must not expect verifiable, objective answers:

> If we ask why the world is the way it is and then ask why
> that answer is the way it is, at the end of this chain of explanations
> we shall find a few simple principles of compelling beauty.[161]

Yet this is not all: the manifold beauty that lies beneath the surface of things is a beckoning from an ultimately beautiful "final theory". Glimpses of beauty in nature are "an anticipation, a premonition" (Weinberg, 165) of an ultimate truth in which all scientific theories culminate.

Philosopher of science Karl Popper bracketed the aesthetic principle and favored instead a stark empiricism that left no room for "ultimate explanations."[162] As limited intellectual beings, he argues, we can only propose theories that participate in higher, more universal theories. There is no explanation, Popper concludes, that isn't itself completed by a more inclusive explanation. Other scientists reason, on a more humble note, that humans are simply not intelligent enough to recognize or comprehend a final theory. Weinberg is in the minority in his persistent hope for a valid final theory. He prefers to journey with Ulysses, to "follow knowledge like a sinking star, beyond

---
[161] Weinberg, p. 165.
[162] K. R. Popper. Objective Knowledge: An Evolutionary Approach. Oxford: Clarendon Press, 1972, p. 195.

the utmost bounds of human thought... beyond the sunset, and the baths of all the western stars."[163] To enlist in this quest is ultimately more human, he believes, than to abandon the quest itself in the name of reason.

---

[163] Alfred Lord Tennyson, "Ulysses," The Works of Alfred Lord Tennyson, Poet Laureate. New York: Grosset &

CONCLUSION

Julia Kristeva and Gaston Bachelard construct categories of knowledge and models of subjectivity that demystify classical notions of truth, objectivity, and reality. The literary and psychoanalytic theories of Kristeva acknowledge transcendence even as they tear down metaphysical categories of absolute truth and identity. Bachelard's "new scientific mind" and archetypal poetics offer fresh perspectives on classical physics and literary criticism, while leaving room for a revamped, modem absolute. The central concern for both thinkers is the need for a new epistemology, one that proposes an intertextuality of the irrational and the discursive, the imaginary and the theoretical.

For Kristeva, the question is framed on many levels: she first seeks a language of "semanalysis" that would incorporate the semiotic drive impulses without falling prey to the non-sense of radical negativity. Disillusioned by scientism and its self-professed mastery of nature, then by politics, where she finds the individual eclipsed by the power of the state, Kristeva looks to psychoanalytic theory for a dialectical resolution of the imaginary and the scientific.

(cont) Dunlap, 1906, p. 94.

The self, for Kristeva, is both a prisoner of the *chora,* conditioned by the semiotic drive impulses that bind it to the maternal body, and a creative subject-in-process that is intimately involved in the production of meaning. The construction of identity and the autonomy of the self is a product of the dialectical "doublebind"[164] of which critic Oliver Kelly speaks: there are traces of the symbolic, archaic patterns of meaning, present in the semiotic just as there are echoes of the body present in the propositions of language.

Given the mutuality of the semiotic and the symbolic, for Kristeva there can be no monolithic, absolute truth. Truth is an emerging process of intertextuality that is infinitely self-generating. The precursor of meaning - the mother-child dyad - is incorporated into the figure of the Imaginary Father, where neither the negativity of the drives nor the constructs of language prevail. Abject literature, as exemplified in much of avant-garde poetry, engages language to tell the tale of the subject in exile from its maternal origins, always *on the way* to making itself whole again through the cathartic release of negativity in poetry.

While Kristeva rejects the notion of an absolute in language--the subject-in-process can never "speak the unspeakable" and is conditioned by both his symbolic and his semiotic legacy—she leaves room for a metaphysics of sorts. The experience of the "sublime" as that "something else that expands us..."

---

[164] Oliver Kelly. Reading Kristeva: Unraveling the Doublebind. Bloomington: Indiana University Press, 1993.

(Powers, 12) as we attempt to translate the experience of the semiotic into language is a curious admixture of transcendence and immanence – an absolute from within. Only the language of the imagination, the "mother tongue," can capture the allure and the estrangement, the "dazzling obscurity" (Smith, 30) of the "sentiment of the body" (Kristeva, The Speaking Subject, 1985). The poetic word is able to pierce the "veil of representation" (RPL 103) that shields ordinary discourse; a new language, infused with negativity and the archaic phonemes of the proto-subject, captures the voice of the semiotic. Yet this voice of the subject-in-process never has the last word: the "infinitisation of meaning" (RPL 613) can never be contained within the confines of language. The text is but a "linguistic fabric" (RPL 542-543) of many threads, each one defying the predictable patterns of meaning and replacing them with "plural and heterogeneous universes (Kristeva, Semeiotike, 14). For Kristeva, much like the young critics at Iena, the modern absolute is the very *process* itself of signification, never a final *Aufhebung* - always "plural, heterogeneous, and contradictory...."[165]

The subject, by confronting its own rootedness in the semiotic, experiences both the ecstasy of *jouissance*- a sort of reunion with the maternal body and its nourishing pleasures--and the "basic incompleteness" (Powers, 88-89) caused by abjection. It is psychoanalysis that allows the subject to

---

[165] Kristeva. Revolution in Poetic Language, Kelly Oliver, ed., The Portable Kristeva. NY: Columbia University Press, 1997, p. 59.

theorize this paradox of joyful emptiness. The imaginary constructs of the analytic dialogue-a meeting ground of art ("the alchemy of the word" (Kolocotroni, 165)) and science (the "universal syntax" (Powers, 196)-allow the subject to encounter a "mystical metamorphosis" - a glimpse of the modern absolute.

Bachelard frames the question of the absolute against the backdrop of science in the age of relativity. If even science, that most empirically verifiable of disciplines, must question what constitutes reality and its mode of knowing, then surely philosophy and literature must follow suit. Just as Kristeva shifted the parameters of science to allow for infinite meaning, randomness, and pleasure[166] so Bachelard finds that the "new scientific mind" can do no more than approximate a final truth. Absolute certainty is a chimera for the modern scientist, who must yield to the increasing role of the imaginary and the intuitive in his search for truth. Ironically, the frustrated quest of modern science and its modified 'probable' truth restores the very metaphysics that science sought to eradicate. The unknown, like Kristeva's "other" or "stranger within," remains the goal of scientific inquiry: by endowing the scientific project with a sense of the poetic, the rational and the imaginary, two poles of the human

---

[166] For example, in the science of semiotics which is "both less and more" than a science in its "pulverization" of meaning, and through the science of psychoanalysis that weaves the texts of the imaginary and the rational in an effort to create a meaning that is true for both self and other.

psyche, join forces in glimpsing the absolute. The Bachelardian "project" is

an epistemological category that conceptualizes the interdependence of subject and object. Since both are defined in terms of each other, science can no longer speak of a given reality over and against the observing subject. The scientific "project" that Bachelard substitutes for the dualism of subject and object becomes Kristeva's project: the conversation of analyst and analysand. The "subject-in-process," by engaging in a dialogue with another (the analyst as "object"), comes to terms with his estrangement and constructs a language that is at once poetic and scientific, imaginative and rational.

Where Kristeva and Bachelard differ, perhaps, is in their qualification of language, or theory, in the pursuit of the absolute. For Kristeva, the ecstatic state of *jouissance* is attained in and through the therapeutic session, where imaginary language and semiotic wordplay alternate with the interjection of theory and symbolic propositions. For Bachelard, the absolute is a hyper-intellectual state of contemplation. "Cogito-cubed", that state of pure consciousness that is "transcended by *difference latent within...* (italics mine)"(Jones, 62) seems to mimic Kristeva's metaphysics of the body. Yet while the Kristevan absolute is encountered in fleeting visions through abject literature, where the mother-tongue is restored, and through the imaginary dialogue of analysis, for Bachelard "spiritualized" being reaches a "special kind of happiness" (Jones, 69) through the discipline of thought that is critically conscious of itself. Although Bachelard qualifies this a-temporal zone of consciousness as an "aesthetic" activity of the mind, it is nevertheless an aesthetic "kind of *thought* (italics mine)" (Jones, 70).

Even in his poetics, where imagination, through literary "effusion" (PR, 45-47), captures the essence of our material being (the "mother-substance" (PS, xxxiv)) Bachelard assigns an archetypal substance to each of the four material images. The faculty of the imagination cannot indulge in spontaneous association, as in the case of Kristeva, in order to uncover these four psychic truths. It is only by "think(ing) matter" (AS, 14) that the absolute joy of a "happy being" (Gaudin, xxvii) is experienced. There is always and already a metaphysical unity between mind and the deeper reality of matter. It takes the imagination, guided by the rigor of the intellect, to unlock the correspondence that unites objects with the "...deepest organic aspects of consciousness" (TR, 81). And although Bachelard recognizes, like Kristeva, that the material level is endowed with meaning "in the direction of depth, and in the direction of height" (ER, 1-4),[167] its meaning is released only through a "truly intellectual lyric state" (DD, 148-150). Furthermore, while Bachelard seems to temper his rationalism by locating the source of poetic truth somewhere

---

[167] As noted above, Kristeva determines that there is inchoate meaning at the deeper level of the semiotic as well as in the higher, rational level of the symbolic.

between the unconscious and the rational (the semiotic and the symbolic), in the "intermediate zone" (PF, 26, 32), it is ultimately an imagination that is "intellectually charged", a reverie that is driven by thought, that alone can transcend the phenomenal world.

Kristeva and Bachelard profess a common understanding of the absolute as a transcendent force that radicalizes traditional notions of matter and mind, imagination and reason, affectivity and intellect. But whereas Kristeva limits the scope of the subject's knowledge to the human psyche in its infinite development, Bachelard embraces a new metaphysics—a poetics—that uncovers the "relatedness" (Gaudin, 118) of being itself. In this sense, then, the Kristevan absolute can be seen as a psycho-social process, while Bachelard endows the absolute with an ontological status. Both in the "spiritual exercise" (RA, 77-81) of the scientific mind as it encounters the limits of reason, and in the transforming "verticality" (Gaudin, 161) of poetry, language drives the human spirit to "...something beyond ourselves..." (Gaudin, 172).

Contemporary cosmology grapples with the dilemma of ultimate truth in the form of an epistemological absolute or "final theory". It arrives at the conclusion that if there is a Theory of Everything to be formulated, it is to be done through a process that is both predictable and irrational. Often, the principles of reason are exhausted by a "noumenal something else" which only an aesthetic inquiry can uncover. Modern science, in the tradition of Kristeva and Bachelard, has become "art" – weaving fictional tales of truth, making room for the chaotic, the noisy, and the unreal as so many unravelings of the Absolute.

BIBLIOGRAPHY

Appignanesi, L., ed. "Julia Kristeva in Conversation with Rosalind Coward." **Desire.** London: ICA Documents, 1984.

Atlan, Henri, "Disorder, Complexity and Meaning," **Disorder and Order,** ed. P. Livingston. Stanford:1984.

"Bachelard, Gaston." **The Encylopedia of Philosophy.** New York: Macmillan Publishing Co., Inc. & The Free Press, 1984.

Bachelard, Gaston. **L'Activite rationaliste de la physique contemporaine.** Paris: Presses Universitaires de France, 1951.

—. **La Dialectique de la duree.** Paris: P.U.F., 1936.

Essai sur la connaissance approchee. Paris: J. Vrin, 1938.

Etude sur revolution d'un probleme de physique: la propagation thermique dans les solides. Paris: J. Vrin, 1928.

Les Intuitions atomistiques (Essai de classification). Paris: J. Win, 1975.

Lautreamont. Paris: Jose Cort, 1939.

Le Materialisme rationnel. Paris: P.U.F., 1953.

Le Nouvel Esprit scientifique. Paris: Alcan, 1934.

La Philosophie du non: Essai d'une philosophie du nouvel esprit scientifique. Paris: P.U.F., 1940.

—. "The Poetic Moment and the Metaphysical Moment," **The Right to Dream.** New York: Grossman, 1971.

—. **La Poetique de l'espace.** Paris: P.U.F., 1957.

. **La Poetique de la reverie.** Paris: P.U.F., 1960.

La Psychanalyse du feu. Paris: Gallimard, 1938.

—. **Le Rationalisme applique.** Paris: P.U.F., 1949.

—. **La Terre et les reveries de la volonte: Essai sur l'imagination des forces.** Corti, 1948.

La Valeur inductive de la relativite. Paris: J. Vrin, 1929.

Barrow, John and F. Tipler. **The Anthropic Cosmological Principle.** Oxford: Oxford University Press, 1986.

Barrow, John. **Theories of Everything: The Quest for Ultimate Explanation.** Oxford: Clarendon Press, 1991.

Baruch, E. and L. Serrano, ed. "Interview with Julia Kristeva." **Women Analyze Women.** New York: New York University Press, 1988.

Barthes, Roland. "L'Etrangere." **La Quinzaine litteraire** 94 (1970): 19.

Blake, William. "Jerhusalem." **The Portable Blake.** Ed. Alfred Kazin. New York: 1976.

Bosco, Henri. **Un Oubli moins profond** Trans. Colette Gaudin. Paris: Gallimard, 1961.

Christofides, C.G. "Bachelard's Aesthetics." **Journal of Aesthetics and Art Criticism** 20 (1962): 267.

Davies, Paul. **The Mind of God.** New York: Simon and Schuster, 1992.

—. **Superforce: The Search for a Grand Unified Theory of Nature.** New York: Simon & Schuster, 1984.

De Man, Paul. "The Resistance to Theory." **Yale French Studies** 63 (1982): 15.

Derrida, Jacques. "Difference." **Speech and Phenomena and Other Essays on Husserl's Theory of Signs.** Evanston: Northwestern University Press, 1974.

—. **Of Grammatology.** Baltimore: Johns Hopkins University Press, 1976.

Durand, Gilbert. **Les Structures anthropologiques de l'imaginaire.** Paris:

Bordas, 1969.

Easlea, Brian. **Science and Sexual Oppression.**

Ferriere, Gabriele. "Jean Cavailles, philosophe et combattant (1903-1944)." **L'Engagement rationaliste.** By Gaston Bachelard. Paris: P.U.F., 1972. 178-190.

Gagey, Jacques. **Gaston Bachelard ou la conversion a l'imaginaire.** Paris: Marcel Riviere, 1969.

Garin, Eugenio. **L'Education de l'homme moderne.** Paris: 1968.

Gaudin, Colette. "L'Imagination et le reverie: Remarques sur la poetique de Gaston Bachelard." **Symposium** 20. (1966): xi.

Hadamard, Jacques. **The Psychology of Invention in the Mathematical** Field. Princeton: Princeton University Press, 1949.

Hartle, James. "Excess Baggage." **Particle Physics and the Universe: Essays in Honour of Gell-Mann.**

Hawking, Stephen. **A Brief History of lime.** New York: Bantam Books, 1988.

Heidegger, Martin. "The End of Philosophy and the Task of Thinking." **Basic Writings.** New York: Harper & Row, 1977.

. "The Question of Being." **Basic Writings.** New York: Harper & Row, 1977.

Henderson, L.J. **The Fitness of the Environment.** Reprinted Peter Smith. Gloucester, Massachusetts, 1970.

Horgan, John. **The End of Science.** London: Little, Brown & Company, 1996.

Husserl, Edmund. **Ideas: General Introduction to Pure Phenomenology.** London: Allen and Unwin, 1931.

Jones, Mary McAllester. **Gaston Bachelard, Subversive Humanist.** Madison: University of Wisconsin Press, 1991.

Kant, Immanuel. **Critique of Pure Reason.** 1787. London: Macmillan, 1929.

Kelly, Oliver. **Reading Kristeva: Unraveling the Doublebind.** Bloomington: Indiana University Press, 1993.

Kolocotroni, Vassiliki. "Julia Kristeva." **Textual Practice** 5 (1991): 165.

Korzybski, Alfred. **Science and Sanity: An Introduction to Non-Aristotelian Systems and General Semantics.** New York: The International Non-Aristotelian Library Company, 1933.

Kurweil, Edith. "An Interview with Julia Kristeva." **Partisan Review** 53 (1986): 297.

Kristeva, Julia. **Black Sun.** New York: Columbia University Press, 1989.

—. **Les Cahiers du GRIF** 32.

—. **Desire in Language: a Semiotic Approach to Literature and Art.** Oxford: Blackwell. New York: Columbia University Press, 1984.

Etranger a nous-memes. Paris: Fayard, 1988.

—. **Le Langage, cet inconnu.** Paris: Editions du Seuil, 1981.

—."Un Nouveau type d'intellectuel: le dissident." **Tel Quel** 74 (1977): 300.

—. **Pouvoirs de l'horreur.** Paris: Seuil, 1980.

—. **Powers of Horror.** New York: Columbia University Press, 1982.

—. **La Revolution du langage poetique.** Paris: Editions du Seuil, 1974.

—. **Revolution in Poetic Language.** Trans. Margaret Waller. New York: Columbia University Press, 1993.

—.**Semeiotike: Recherches pour une Semanalyse.** Paris: Editions du Seuil, 1969.

—. **Soleil Noir.** Paris: Gallimard, 1987.

—. "Le Sujet en proces." **Polylogue.** Paris: Seuil, 1977.

—. "The System and the Speaking Subject." **The Tell-Tale Sign: A Survey of Semiotics.** Ed. Thomas A. Sebeok. Lisse, Netherlands: The Peter de Ridder Press, 1975.

—. **Le Texte du roman.** The Hague: Mouton, 1970.

—. **Le Vieil homme et les loups.** Paris: Fayard, 1991.

Landauer, Rolf. "Computation and Physics: Wheeler's Meaning Circuit?" **Foundations of Physics** 16 (1986): 551.

Lotman, Juni. "The Structure of the Artistic Text." Trans. G. Lenhoff and R. Vroon. **Michigan Slavic Contributions** 7 (1977): 75.

Lyotard, Jean-Francois. **The Postmodem Condition.** Trans. G. Bennington and B. Massumi. Minneapolis: University of Minnesota Press, 1974.

Michelson, A. "The Day Appears Not Far Distant." **Light Waves and Their** Uses. Chicago: University of Chicago Press, 1903.

Midgley, Mary. **Science as Salvation: A Modem Myth and its Meaning.** London: Routlege, 1994.

Moi, Toril, ed. **The Kristeva Reader.** New York: Columbia University Press, 1986.

Monod, Jacques. **Chance and Necessity.** Trans. A. Wainhouse. London: Collins, 1972.

Nasr, S.H. "Spirituality and Science—Convergence or Divergence?" **Sophia** 1(0akton, Virginia: The Foundation for Traditional Studies, 1995).

Oliver, Kelly. **Reading Kristeva.** Indianapolis: Indiana University Press, 1993.

Peat, David. **The Philosopher's Stone: The Sciences of Synchronicity and Creativity.** New York: Bantam Doubleday, 1991.

Paulson, W.R. **The Noise of Culture.** Ithaca: Cornell University Press, 1988.

Penrose, Roger. **The Emperor's New Mind: Concerning Computers, Minds and the Laws of Physics.** Oxford: Oxford University Press, 1989.

Plato. "Timaeus." Trans. F. Comford. **Revolution in Poetic Language.** By Julia Kristeva. New York: Columbia University Press, 1984. 239.

Polkinghorne, John. "The Faith of a Physicist." **Physics Education** 22 (1987): 22.

Popper, Karl. **Objective Knowledge: An Evolutionary Approach.** Oxford: Clarendon Press, 1972.

Prigogine, Ilya and Isabelle Stengers. **La Nouvelle Alliance: Metamorphose de la science.** Paris: Gallimard, 1979.

—. **Order Out of Chaos.** New York: Bantam Books, 1984.

Redhead, M. **From Physics to Metaphysics.** Cambridge: Cambridge University Press, 1996.

Richards, I.A. **Science and Poetry.** New York: Norton, 1926.

Rose, Jacqueline. "Julia Kristeva: Take Two." **Jacqueline Rose: Sexuality in the Field of Vision.** London: NLB/Verso, 1986.

Rucker, Rudy. **Infinity and the Mind.** Boston: Birkhauser, 1987.

Schlegel, Friedrich. "Critical Fragment 115." **"Lucinde" and the Fragments.** Trans. P. Firchow. Minneapolis: University of Minnesota Press, 1971.

Serres, Michel. **Genese.** Paris: Gallimard, 1982.

—. **The Parasite.** Trans. LR. Schehr. Baltimore: 1982.

—. **Hermes: Literature, Science, Philosophy.** Eds. D.F. Bell and J.V. Harari. Baltimore: Johns Hopkins University Press, 1982.

Shelley, Percy B. **Shelley's Prose.** Ed. D.L. Clark. Albuquerque, 1954.

Smith, Anna. **Julia Kristeva: Readings of Exile and Estrangement.** New York: St. Martin's Press, 1966.

Snow, C.P. **The Two Cultures and the Scientific Revolution.** Cambridge, 1959.

Stannard, Russell. **Grounds for Reasonable Belief.** Edinburgh: Scottish Academic Press, 1989.

—. "No Faith in the Grand Theory." **The limes.** London: 13 Nov. 1989.

Stengers, Isabelle. "Decouvrir la complexite?" **Ordres et desordres: Enquete sur un nouveau paradigme.** Paris, 1982.

Stockwood, Mervyn, ed. **Religion and the Scientists.** London: SCM, 1959.

Tennyson, Alfred Lord. "Ulysses," **The Works of Alfred Lord Tennyson, Poet Laureate.** New York: Grosset & Dunlap, 1906.

Thom, Rene. "Stop Chance! Stop Noise!" Trans. R. Chumbley. **SubStance** 40 (1983): 11.

Torrance, Thomas. **Divine and Contingent Order.** Oxford: Oxford University Press, 1981.

Vadee, Michel. **Bachelard ou le nouvel idealisme epistemologique.** Paris: Editions Sociales, 1975.

Valery, Paul. **Le Cimetiere marin.** Ed. Graham D. Martin. Austin: University of Texas Press, 1971.

Weinberg, Steven. **Dreams of a Final Theory.** New York: Vintage Books, 1993.

—. **The First Three Minutes.** London: Andre Deutsch, 1977

Wheeler, John. "Information, Physics, Quantum: The Search for Links." **Complexity, Entropy and the Physics of Information.** Ed. Wojciech H. Zurek and Addison-Wesley. Redwood City, California, 1990.

Whitehead, Alfred North. **Science and the Modern World.** New York: Macmillan Publishing Co., Inc., 1925.

Wigner, Eugene. **Communications in Pure and Applied Mathematics** 13 (1960): 1.

Woolf, Virginia. **Moments of Being.** Grafton: Hammersmith, 1989.

VDM publishing house ltd.

Scientific Publishing House

offers

free of charge publication

of current academic research papers, Bachelor´s Theses, Master's Theses, Dissertations or Scientific Monographs

If you have written a thesis which satisfies high content as well as formal demands, and you are interested in a remunerated publication of your work, please send an e-mail with some initial information about yourself and your work to *info@vdm-publishing-house.com.*

Our editorial office will get in touch with you shortly.

VDM Publishing House Ltd.
Meldrum Court 17.
Beau Bassin
Mauritius
www.vdm-publishing-house.com

VDM Verlag Dr. Müller

LAP LAMBERT Academic Publishing

SVH Südwestdeutscher Verlag für Hochschulschriften

Printed in Great Britain by
Amazon.co.uk, Ltd.,
Marston Gate.